Your Lifestyle Guide to

Digital Photography

Second Edition

Gateway™

Notices

Your Lifestyle Guide to Digital Photography, Second Edition

is published by
Gateway, Inc.
14303 Gateway Place
Poway, CA 92064

© 2003 Gateway, Inc.

All Rights Reserved

In the interest of continued product development, Gateway reserves the right to make improvements in this book at any time, without notice or obligation.

Microsoft screen shot(s) reprinted by permission from Microsoft Corporation.

Trademark Acknowledgments

Version 1.0

ISBN: 1-57729-461-0

DATE: 10-14-03

Printed in the United States of America

Distributed in the United States by Gateway, Inc.

Welcome

From the introduction of digital photography in Chapter 1 through sharing and enjoying your images in Chapter 8, *Your Lifestyle Guide to Digital Photography* provides you with what you need to know to shoot, organize, and share your digital photos. This product is designed to accommodate your learning style, and to make learning easy, interesting, and fun. You can stick to just the bare essentials or learn in greater depth by practicing key skills and applying your new knowledge. Our goal is to show you how technology can enhance your life, provide some fun, and open up new opportunities.

Classroom Learning

A hands-on training course on this subject is offered to enhance and improve your skills. Classes are held at Gateway® stores nationwide and additional fees may apply. Our classes are ideal solutions for people who want to become knowledgeable and get up and running in just three hours. They provide the opportunity to learn from one of our experienced and friendly instructors and practice important skills with other students. Call 888-852-4821 for enrollment information. One of our representatives will assist you in selecting a time and location that is convenient for you. If applicable, please have your Gateway customer ID and order number ready when you call. Please refer to your Gateway paperwork for this information.

More Than a Book

Your Lifestyle Guide to Digital Photography is more than a book; it is a blended learning system that also includes a CD-ROM and Internet presentations and activities. These tools all work together to provide a truly unique learning experience. The book presents technical information in visual, practical, and understandable ways. The CD-ROM extends the book by providing additional material on the subject. Continue learning online by logging on to www.LearnwithGateway.com. The enrollment key provided with this book gives you access to additional content and interactive exercises. This Web site allows us to keep you updated on rapidly changing information and new software releases.

Contents

Contents

Contents

How to Use This Book

As you read the chapters in this book, you'll find pictures, figures, and diagrams to help reinforce key ideas and concepts. You'll also find pictures or icons that serve as cues to flag important information or provide directions. Here is a guide to help you understand the icons you'll encounter in this book:

 A Note identifies a relatively important piece of information that will make things easier or faster for you to accomplish on your PC. Most notes are worth reading, if only for the time and effort they can save you.

 A Warning gives notice that an action on your PC can have serious consequences and could lead to loss of work, delays, or other problems. Our goal is not to scare you, but to steer you clear of potential sources of trouble.

You'll find sidebar information spread throughout the chapters, as follows:

> ### More About . . .
> The More About . . . information is supplementary, and is provided so you can learn more about making technology work for you. Feel free to skip this material during your first pass through the book, but please return to it later.

You can use each part of our innovative Survive & Thrive™ learning system by itself, or combine them for the ultimate learning experience.

 Come to a class at your local Gateway® store and enjoy a face-to-face learning experience with one of our expert instructors. Our state-of-the-art facilities and interactive approach are designed to build your new skills quickly – and let you have fun at the same time.

 Learn at your own pace using the enclosed full-color book. It combines high-tech images and concise overviews with simple instructions to create an ideal guide and ongoing reference.

 Enter the exciting world of online learning at www.LearnwithGateway.com, the Web site that delivers high-quality instruction the way you want it, when you want it.

 Immerse yourself in the enclosed CD bonus materials. Simply insert the CD into your PC, and go. That's all it takes to launch the innovative extras we've included.

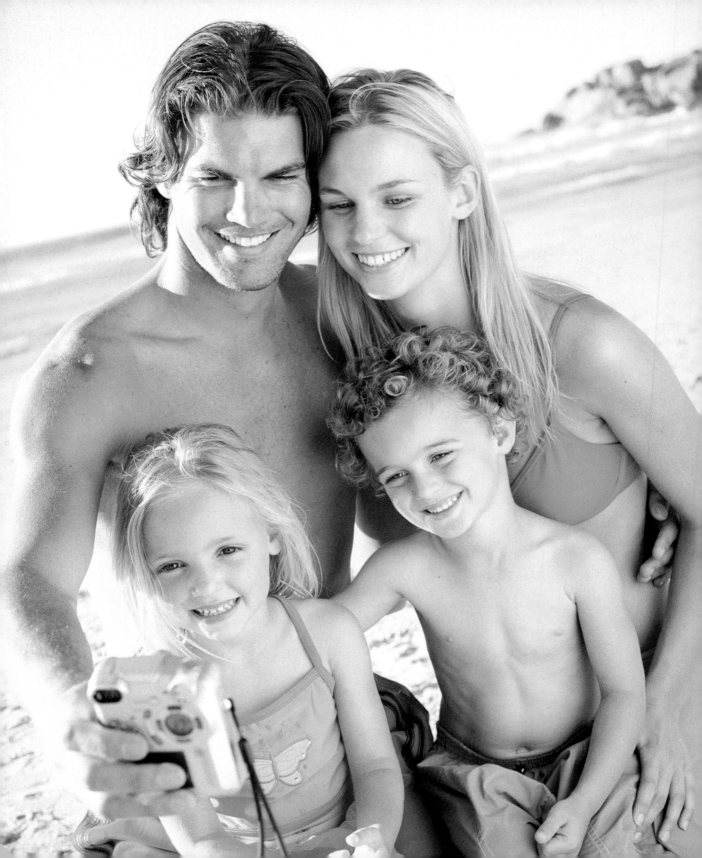

Discovering Digital Photography

Welcome to the exciting world of digital photography! You are about to learn how the digital age has revolutionized the way you capture, view, organize, edit, and share images. Rolls of film, professional darkrooms, and messy chemicals are no longer required to create memories, and that is just the beginning. Improved personal computer technology, the Internet, scanning devices, and digital cameras enable you to stretch the boundaries of traditional photography and do remarkable things that were impossible just a few years ago. Today you can view pictures on your camera's built-in monitor, remove pesky red-eye, print snapshots at home, and do much more. Many software packages provide simple tools that turn static photographic images into exciting works of art. In fact, after you realize the convenience provided by digital cameras and the incredible versatility of digital images, you might even decide to put away your film-based camera for good!

This chapter introduces you to the fundamentals of digital photography. In addition to learning what the phrase "digital photography" means, you'll discover all the fun things you can do with your digital images. You'll also learn about the many sources of digital images, including pictures taken with a digital camera, scanned images, and other sources. You'll also learn about the many advantages of working with digital images. With digital photography, you can e-mail photos, create a snapshot book, order prints online, and more. Later chapters will cover in detail how to accomplish all this!

Traditional vs. Digital Photography: What's the Difference?

The easiest way to describe digital photography is to compare a digital camera to a traditional camera. In fact, digital cameras are quite similar to their film-based counterparts, given that they include such familiar features as lenses, flashes, and shutters. So what's the difference? The obvious one is that digital cameras don't use film to record the scene you are photographing. Instead, they use sensors or arrays called CCDs (Charge-Coupled Devices) that convert light information from the photographed scene into a digital image.

Digital images are made up of individual picture elements called pixels. A pixel is a tiny dot of light that is the basic unit of images on a computer screen or in a digital image. These pixels combine to make the picture, and they are stored together as a digital file. Digital images can come from many sources, one of which is from digital cameras.

A digital camera works a lot like your computer; it converts the image you are photographing into a digital file. You can then use this digital file in many ways. (See "Taking Advantage of Digital Images" later in this chapter.)

The digital image is stored as a file in your camera's memory or on a memory card (a removable disk that is similar to a computer floppy disk, but smaller). Then you can transfer the image to your computer. The number of pictures you can store will vary depending on the amount of available memory in your camera or on a memory card, as well as the resolution of the images and the level of compression. Since higher-resolution images contain more pixels, the files containing the images are larger and thus consume more space in your camera's memory or on your memory card.

The quality of a picture, called its resolution, is a measure of the number of pixels per inch. The more pixels per inch an image contains, the better the image quality. Minimizing the file size is called compression. Electronic images are compressed automatically so more will fit into the camera's storage device. The higher the compression, the smaller the file sizes; however, at higher compression rates detail is lost from the image. You'll learn more about image quality and compression in Chapter 2, "Exploring Photography Hardware."

Once you've filled the memory in your digital camera or on your memory card, you simply copy the images from your camera to your computer in a process called downloading. Then you can delete the images from the camera's memory or memory card, and voila, you're ready to take more pictures. You never need to pay for film again!

 Throughout this book, when you see the phrase "digital image," it refers to pictures or illustrations from any one of these sources, not just pictures taken with a digital camera. Pictures taken with a digital camera are also referred to as digital pictures or photographs.

Why Go Digital?

Now that you have a good idea of what digital photography is, you can add up all the advantages. Doing so can help you evaluate whether it's worth purchasing a digital camera. If you already have one, you can get a better understanding of how this new piece of equipment, and the electronic images it produces, can make photography easier and more versatile. The following sections detail some key advantages of using a digital camera, and the benefits of working with electronic image files instead of traditional prints.

Preview Pictures Immediately

On a digital camera, you can preview your pictures immediately after you take them. If you've ever picked up a set of pictures at your photo shop, eagerly anticipating your capture of that once-in-a-lifetime moment on film, only to discover blurry prints of what might be your parents dancing at their fiftieth wedding anniversary, you'll appreciate this feature. Most digital cameras, such as the MinoltaDiMAGExt shown in Figure 1-1, feature a color LCD (Liquid Crystal Display) monitor on the back that

Figure 1-1 View pictures as you take them with a built-in LCD display, standard on most digital cameras.

displays each picture immediately after you take it. If the picture isn't good, you can discard it and take it again.

No Film or Negatives Required

Because your pictures are stored in a digital format in the camera's memory or on the camera's memory card, you can copy the pictures to your computer, clear them from memory, and take new shots. You can also use your digital camera's controls to delete unwanted pictures at any time. Because you can store and organize all of your images on your computer, you never have to hunt through negatives to produce additional prints.

Organize Photos on Your Computer

As shown in Figure 1-2, you can use a simple connection to transfer digital images from your camera directly to your computer. Then, you can take advantage of all the helpful benefits your computer provides to manage them. You can organize images in folders, delete or rename them, or search for image files using the Microsoft® Windows® search function. You can also use other software programs to create albums and slideshows easily.

Figure 1-2 Easily transfer images from your digital camera directly to your computer.

Share Digital Images Online

You can e-mail photos of your new baby to your sister in Antarctica, or you can include photos on your Web page or in a document. Professional photographers especially benefit from this feature because they can quickly broadcast their work to their customers. Sharing your images online is covered in more detail in Chapter 8, "Sharing and Enjoying Your Images."

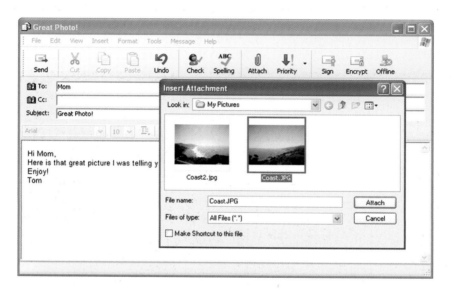

Scan Existing Photographs

Have a collection of photos that you want to store on your computer? You can scan these photos and convert them into digital images. Your old photos can now benefit from all of the same advantages as photos taken with a digital camera.

Edit Your Own Photographs

If you find some minor flaws in a photograph or you need to resize it, it's no problem. You can choose from a variety of software programs, such as Adobe® Photoshop Elements (shown in Figure 1-3), that are designed specifically to edit and enhance digital images. Crop images to a smaller size, remove red-eye, apply color effects, and perform other functions to improve your photos. In addition, you can use the software tools to repair traditional photographs after you have scanned and saved them on your computer, and you can use a variety of effects to generate interesting manipulations of the original image.

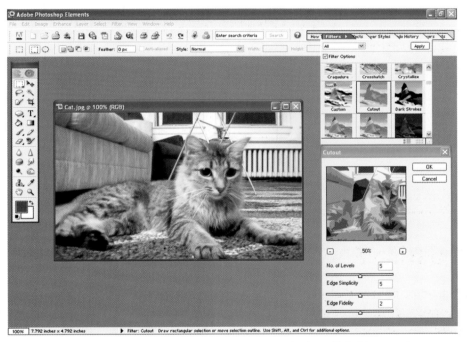

Figure 1-3 You can use image editor programs to manipulate digital images in many ways.

Choose from Additional Printing Options

Because you have the ability to preview an image, you can print only the desired images using your own printer or a special photo-quality printer. Alternatively, you can order prints online. If you are loyal to your local photo shop, you can take your images there and have them create the prints. More options ensure that you get what you want when you want it.

Also, the ability to generate traditional prints from digital images gives you additional control over your photographs. If you commonly order double prints when you develop film from your traditional camera, you inevitably end up with 20 extra pictures you don't really need. With a digital camera, you can select not just the quantity of each print, but also the size, including 5×7s, wallets, and others.

Easy to Learn and Economical

Once you learn the features of your digital camera and the basics for managing images, you have the ability to do almost anything you can do with a conventional camera. Because you never have to purchase film, the more pictures you take, the more you benefit from going digital. In addition, prices for digital cameras and scanners have gotten so low that buying one of these devices is more affordable than ever.

Discovering Many Sources of Digital Images

Using today's technology, there are many ways to acquire, store, and transfer digital images. Therefore, you can find them everywhere. Just do a quick Internet search, and

you'll find thousands of images of just about anything imaginable. Of course, most important is that creating your own digital images is easier than ever before. Using a digital camera is the most common way to produce original digital photos. You'll learn all about taking good pictures using a digital camera in Chapter 3, "Taking Great Pictures."

But using a digital camera isn't the only way to create digital images. In fact, there are several other ways to obtain digital pictures, including scanners, online images, and more. The following list gives you a good idea of the many sources of digital images:

✦ **Using a scanner.** Suppose you're planning to attend a family reunion and you want to create a scrapbook of old family photographs for the other attendees. Instead of paying to have the images reprinted at a photo shop, you can use a scanner, like the one shown in Figure 1-4, to copy the images and save them as files on your computer. Then you can print the images using your own printer. You'll learn more about scanning existing pictures in Chapter 4, "Organizing and Managing Your Images."

Figure 1-4 You can use a scanner to transfer traditional prints to your computer.

✦ **Using a CD.** Many photo developers will place your images on CD when you develop film. You can open these files from the CD and work with them on your computer.

All new computers come with a recordable CD or DVD drive which you can use to record (or burn) your own CDs or DVDs. Because photo files can be quite large, storing them on CDs is a great way to keep your photos organized. You learn more about storing and organizing pictures, including using a recordable CD/DVD drive, in Chapter 6.

✦ **Using the Web.** In addition to placing your images on CD, many photo developers will place your photos on a Web site from which you can view, download, share, and print them. Alternatively, some Web sites offer clip-art illustrations or photographs that you can download and use, as shown in Figure 1-5.

Figure 1-5 You can find many sources of digital images online.

Some images are copyrighted. Just because you find a picture you like on the Web does not mean you have permission to use that image as you see fit. Many clip-art and photo sites spell out what you can and cannot do with their images.

Taking Advantage of Digital Images

Because digital cameras are easy to use and provide immediate results and endless editing capabilities, professional photographers were among the first to welcome digital photography. But even though they were among the first, they aren't the only ones who've found uses for digital cameras. Now you'll explore some examples of using digital photography for your business or family photographs and documents.

In addition to highlighting some uses for digital images, this section will also discuss some of the techniques for enhancing or repairing pictures using special photo-editing software.

Photo Possibilities

Digital photos are easy to transfer to your computer, and you can use them in countless different ways. Here are just a few ideas to get your creative wheels turning for your own photographic works.

✦ **Slideshows and albums.** You can combine your pictures into a slideshow or use a picture album on your computer to organize your photos. You can also burn these slideshows and albums to a CD or DVD and even view them on your home entertainment center using a special type of DVD player.

◆ **Web pages.** Liven up your personal or business Web page with photographs. For example, you can showcase your best-selling products on your business site or include pictures of your pet on your personal page. If online auctions are your passion, you'll want to include one or more good pictures of the item you want to sell. Your imagination and the possibilities offered by the Web are limitless!

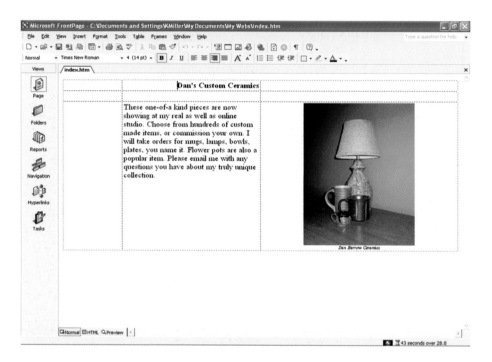

◆ **Online auctions.** If you ever list items for sale on an online auction site, a digital camera can be a great investment. In a matter of minutes, you can take a picture of the item you are selling and post it to your page. Showcasing your item with a digital image attracts potential buyers who generally want to see the condition of an item before placing their bids.

✦ **Family scrapbooks.** Scrapbooking is one of the latest crazes. Just visit any craft store and you'll see aisles and aisles of supplies. With a scanner or camera (or both), you can organize your photographic memories so they tell a story. Using digital images, you can create a highlight book of your children's school years or surprise your parents with a family history that includes scanned photographs of their storied past.

✦ **Craft projects.** In addition to printed projects such as invitations, you can also use your pictures for craft projects. For example, you can apply your images to memory quilts, T-shirts, mugs, and so on.

 Many craft projects require that you print your images on special transfer paper. You can find this paper—as well as craft-related computer programs—at a variety of locations, including hobby or craft stores, computer outlets, office supply stores, or even general purpose retail stores.

+ **Cards, invitations, and banners.** With digital images, you can design your own holiday letter and include pictures of the family. Having a party? Create a fun invitation using digital photos or make a banner for an office party with photos of everyone in the company. You can create many types of documents for entertainment and other purposes!

+ **Business reports.** Pictures are a great way to improve the content and readability of many business reports, including newsletters, annual reports, and more. Do you want your clients to get to know you? Include your picture. Do you need to share a complex plan or diagram with customers? Scan it and then include it in the document. Regardless of your business, you can dress up reports by including photographs.

- **Business cards.** Personalize your business card by adding your picture or company logo. By including your picture, you make sure the recipient will remember your smiling face.

- **Product sales sheets and brochures.** If you are in sales, the old adage "a picture is worth a thousand words" couldn't be truer. You can show your potential clients one or several pictures! For example, realtors use digital images to prepare virtual tours of the homes they're selling—providing a picture of hardwood floors and built-in bookcases makes for an easier sale than simply describing these features.

Scientists and doctors use digital images to photograph microscopic subjects to study them in detail. Digital photography is even used in space. The Hubble Space Telescope, for instance, takes digital images that are then sent back to the space center and distributed to astronomers and the news media.

More About . . . Uses for Digital Photos

For insurance purposes, it's a good idea to keep a list of all your major possessions. That way, in case of a catastrophe, you have a record of the items that may have been lost or damaged. A digital camera is a perfect tool for this project; you can use it to photograph your belongings and insert the images into the document containing your list!

Editing Possibilities

In addition to the many uses for digital images, you also have a great deal of freedom in working with your digital pictures. The programs that enable you to edit digital images are called image-editing programs.

If you own a digital camera, it probably came with its own editing program, which you can use to manipulate your photos. Alternatively, you can purchase programs created by other companies if your needs are more advanced. Although the details of photo-editing software are covered in Chapter 5, "Editing and Manipulating Your Images," following is a quick overview of the types of things you can do with photo-editing programs.

- If your photos have flaws, such as red-eye, you can correct them. You can also remove blemishes and wrinkles, giving yourself or a friend a virtual facelift!

✦ You can crop out portions of the picture to frame your subject better.

✦ You can change the orientation of the image, flipping or rotating it.

✦ You can apply special effects, such as converting a color image to black and white or warping the image.

✦ You can repair old pictures that are torn or stained.

✦ You can manipulate pictures or add and combine them to create a totally new picture. For instance, suppose your friend cannot attend your wedding. You can take an existing photo of your friend and place him or her in a wedding picture, just as if he or she were there!

Digital Photography without a Computer

Ideally, you have a computer on which to copy, edit, and print your pictures. But if you don't, you can still access many of the features and fun of a digital camera. For example, your digital camera's display acts as a portable photo album, so you can view and show off all the pictures (or even the short movies) you've recently taken. Also, some cameras come with removable media, such as CompactFlash and the SmartMedia cards. You can take pictures, store them on these media cards, and then take them to a local print shop. You can also purchase printers that will read media cards and print the images from the card directly without the need for a computer.

What's New in Digital Photography

Manufacturers have greatly improved the quality and feature set available on consumer-model digital cameras, especially compared to early models. For starters, the resolution and sharpness of an image produced by the latest digital cameras are comparable to or better than that of a traditional photograph. Today's digital cameras are leaps and bounds beyond first-generation digital cameras of a comparable price. These devices have also become smarter; you just turn the camera on and press the button. The camera has already adjusted to the light conditions, so you'll likely end up with a great-looking picture.

Technology has improved more than just photo quality. With certain models, you can save (or stamp) data to an image, including the date, time, shutter speed, whether the flash was used, and more. Although including the date and time on the actual print is nothing new, the expanded amount of data saved behind the scenes is valuable when it comes time for you or a photo processor to print the image. Some cameras can even use data from a global positioning system to record the exact place you were on the planet when the picture was taken!

Recently, digital cameras have started showing up as peripherals on portable devices such as PDAs and cellular phones. This capability houses tremendous potential. You can take pictures, view them with the device's monitor, and send them to another compatible phone or PDA. You can even e-mail the image to a friend on the spot. If the advancements of recent years are any indication of the future, you can expect to see more amazing breakthroughs soon. You'll explore these and other exciting prospects in Chapters 2 and 8.

Exploring Photography Hardware

Y ou may be intrigued enough about digital photography to start composing your shopping list, or maybe you've made your purchase already and you're ready to go. Either way, this chapter provides an overview of all the hardware components you need, including the type of computer that works best for digital photography. Later chapters will go into more detail about each component. If you're thinking about purchasing, read this chapter to gain a good understanding of each type of component and the differences between them. If you already have your equipment, consider reading this chapter to learn more about your components. You might decide to purchase more equipment, or discover features on your own camera you hadn't even noticed!

Preparing Your Computer for Digital Photography

As you know, a key component of digital photography—in addition to the digital camera or scanner you use to obtain images—is your computer. To use your camera or scanner

with your computer, it must meet certain system requirements. For example, it must have a CPU (Central Processing Unit) that is powerful enough to work with digital images. In addition, you need enough RAM (Random Access Memory) and hard drive space to run image-editing software and store your collection of images. You also need a DVD or CD (Compact Disc) drive, as well as the right type of connector on your computer for your camera or scanner. Finally, the operating system on your computer must be able to support the use of cameras or scanners.

Both cameras and scanners have varying system requirements. To find out your camera or scanner's requirements, check the packaging or the detailed product information that came with the device.

 If a computer exceeds the minimum system requirements, the performance will be better. In fact, manufacturers sometimes list recommended system requirements that indicate the system properties needed for optimal performance. If this is the case, it is always best for a computer to meet or exceed the recommended requirements.

Finding Your System Information

If you're not sure about your computer's setup (that is, the types of hardware components it uses, its amounts of RAM and hard-drive space, and so on), look at the paperwork from the computer manufacturer or seller. It should list all the components with detailed information for each one. If you can't find your paperwork, follow these steps to get specific hardware information:

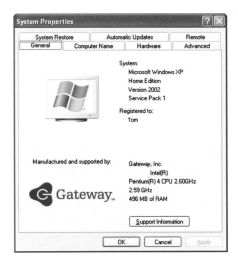

1. Click the start button.
2. Right-click My Computer and then click on Properties in the shortcut menu that appears. The System Properties dialog box will open with the General tab displayed. This tab lists the Windows version, processor type and speed, and amount of RAM for your system.
3. Click the Hardware tab.

4. Click Device Manager. The Device Manager window opens, listing all the devices on your computer, including hard drives, DVD drives, and CD drives.
5. To get detailed information about any of the devices on your computer, click the plus sign next to that device's type.
6. When you've found the device in question, right-click its name, and then choose Properties.

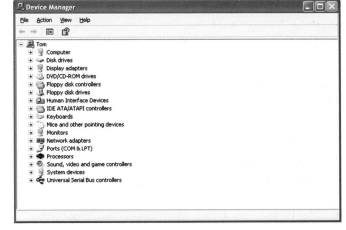

7. The Properties dialog box opens. This dialog box contains several tabs of information about the device. Click the various tabs to gather the information you need.
8. Click OK to close the Properties dialog box.
9. Click the close button to close the Device Manager.
10. Click OK to close the System Properties dialog box.

The CPU

The CPU, shown in Figure 2-1, is the core component of a computer. Sometimes referred to as the brain of the computer, the CPU interprets and carries out instructions, performs all computations, and controls the devices connected to the computer.

A variety of CPUs are available. One well-known manufacturer of CPUs is Intel; another is AMD. Each manufacturer produces various models of CPUs. For example, Intel produces Pentium, Xeon, and Celeron processors, and AMD sells Athlon, Opteron, and Duron processors.

 Laptops often use a different type of processor designed specifically for them.

CPU manufacturers often update their chips, making them faster and more powerful. Also, CPUs have specific names to indicate newer models. For example, a current offering by Intel is the Pentium 4 processor.

In addition to its type, a CPU's speed is important. The CPU's speed is the key factor in the overall speed of the computer. This speed is measured in megahertz (MHz) or gigahertz (GHz). MHz indicates how many million calculations a CPU can perform every second, while GHz indicates how many billion calculations a CPU can perform every second. As you might have guessed, the higher the number, the faster the computer.

The CPU is important when you are working with digital photography because of performance. The processor type and speed determine how quickly you can transfer your images from the camera or scanner to the computer, how quickly you can open and print images, and how long it takes to apply complex effects to photos using image-editing software. Because digital images can be quite large and image-editing software can be demanding, performance is key.

Figure 2-1 The CPU is responsible for processing all of the data used by your computer.

Of course faster is always better, but you don't need a top-of-the-line computer to perform most computing tasks, including digital photography. For example, the Gateway™ DC-T20 requires a Pentium processor of only 166 MHz. Before you purchase a camera, always be sure to confirm that your computer meets the minimum system requirements listed. Also, if you intend to use a particular image-editing program to manipulate your images, check the requirements for the software as well, especially if you are using an older computer. (You can usually find the requirements online.)

RAM

RAM, shown in Figure 2-2, temporarily stores data, software, and the operating system while the computer is operating. RAM is a very important part of a computer; in most

cases, the more RAM a computer has, the better and faster it will perform and the more tasks it can handle at the same time. RAM is measured in megabytes (MB) or gigabytes (GB). A gigabyte is equal to 1,000 megabytes.

Figure 2-2 Data used by software is stored in RAM for easy access by the CPU.

As with CPU speed, the more RAM the better. At the same time, you don't need the highest amount of RAM to enjoy digital photography. The Gateway DC-T20 in this example requires a minimum of 32 MB of RAM (though 64 MB is recommended).

Hard Drive Space

RAM is a temporary storage space where a relatively small amount of information is held as you are working on it. The hard drive is where all of the information on your computer is stored when you are not working on it. Your hard drive is where information is saved permanently, as a file with a particular name, on a specific drive, in a specific folder. Figure 2-3 shows a hard drive. Like RAM, the amount of storage space on your hard drive is measured in megabytes or, more commonly, gigabytes.

Figure 2-3 All programs and files on a computer are stored on the hard drive.

 It's easy to confuse RAM with the hard drive because the two are measured in the same way. Just keep in mind that hard drive space stores information permanently, whereas RAM stores information temporarily. In addition, you have quite a bit more hard drive space than RAM on your computer.

With regard to digital photography, hard drive space is important for the following reasons:

✦ Picture files can be large, so you need plenty of space on your hard drive to store them. You should probably have at least 500 MB or more of free hard drive space.

 In addition to your hard drive, you have other options for storing your files. For example, you can store them on CDs or DVDs. You can also compress your images so they consume less space. Chapter 4, "Organizing and Managing Your Images," goes into more detail about your storage options.

✦ You need space to store the program(s) you use to edit, print, and work with the pictures you create. See the "Selecting an Image Editor" section later in this chapter for more information about these programs.

CD and DVD Drives

Chances are, your camera or scanner will require your computer to have a CD or DVD drive, usually because the software for the device is supplied on a CD or DVD disc. Also, when you install a camera or scanner, Windows uses a special type of file called a driver file, which contains the specific hardware details about your particular device. Drivers are often supplied on CDs as well.

If you can use the drives on your computer to burn CDs or DVDs, you can also use them to store photos. You will learn more about organizing photos on CDs or DVD discs in Chapter 8, "Sharing and Enjoying Your Images."

Cables

One of the most important things to check is how the camera or scanner is connected to your computer. Most connect with a standard USB (Universal Serial Bus) or FireWire cable. You plug one end of the cable into the camera or scanner and the other end into the computer when you want to download or copy images to the computer.

USB system unit port

USB device port

Plugs into system unit port

Plugs into USB device

Most new computers come with several USB ports (generally six) and two or more FireWire ports. If your computer is older, however, it may not have either of these. In that case, consider purchasing a camera that connects using a different type of cable or upgrading your computer to add a USB port.

 Ports are openings like sockets on the back or front of your computer. Older computers typically have one parallel port, which is most often used to connect a printer. These computers also have serial ports (usually two) to connect other devices such as mouses, modems, and so on. Nowadays parallel, serial, and USB ports are standard. FireWire and USB 2.0 are examples of newer types of connections and offer faster data transfer between the external device and your computer.

Operating System

This book discusses digital photography in the context of Windows XP, which includes several handy photo-handling features. For instance, you can plug in your camera, and the Windows plug-and-play feature will automatically install it. When you take pictures, you can connect the camera and download the pictures from the camera to the computer without any other software. Windows XP also includes a special My Pictures folder and some picture-related tasks.

If you are using an earlier version of Windows, however, you don't necessarily need to upgrade. Many versions of Windows provide support for digital photography, but it's a good idea to check your camera or scanner's documentation to make sure your version of Windows will work with the device.

Digital Camera Basics

Just like film-based cameras, digital cameras come in all shapes and sizes and with many different features. The camera that is best for you depends on considerations such as the quality of pictures you need and the amount of money you want to spend. For example, if you're new to photography (digital or otherwise), a general-purpose model will probably suit your needs. Most basic cameras take adequate pictures. If you're more experienced, however, you might want a model with more advanced features. In addition, you should take into account a number of accessories that accompany digital cameras, such as batteries and memory cards for storage, when you step into the world of digital photography.

 If you're thinking of buying a camera, you can use this section to help you select the model that best suits your needs. If you already have a camera, you can read this section to figure out what features it has. You may decide to upgrade your camera as you become more experienced.

It's best to start with a good idea of what you want to accomplish with your camera, and then use the following list to understand the differences among cameras. This list gives you a good idea of what you need to take into consideration when you are choosing a camera.

- Picture quality
- File format
- Camera storage
- Storage media
- Display

- Camera size
- Camera features
- Power source
- Programs included with the camera

Table 2-1 Digital Camera Specifications

CAMERA	GATEWAY DC-T20	NIKON COOLPIX 3100	GATEWAY DC-T50	MINOLTA DiMAGE S414	CANON POWERSHOT G5
Digital Zoom	2 x	4.0x	4x	2.2x	5x
Sensor Resolution (Effective Pixels)	2 million	3.2 million	5 million	4.1 million	5 million
Optical Sensor Size	1/2.7"	1/2.7"	1/2.6"	1/2.15"	1/1.8"
Optical Sensor Type	CMOS	CCD	CCD	CCD	CCD
Light Sensitivity	Auto	ISO 50–200	Auto	ISO 64-400	ISO 50–400
Still Image Format	JPEG	JPEG	JPEG	JPEG	JPEG
Lens Aperture	F/2.8	F/2.8–F/4.9	F/2.8–F/4.8	F/3.0–F/3.6	F2.0–F/3.0
Camera Flash Type	Built-in flash	Built-in flash	Built-in flash	Built-in flash	Built-in flash
Storage Media	SD Memory Card	CompactFlash	SD Memory Card	CompactFlash	CompactFlash
Display Type	TFT color LCD 1.5"	TFT color LCD 1.5"	TFT color LCD 1.5"	TFT color LCD 1.8"	TFT color LCD 1.8"
Weight	3.9 oz	5.3 oz	6.3 oz	11.8 oz	14.5 oz

Where can you find all these details? If you've already bought a camera, this information probably appears somewhere on its packaging. If you're shopping around, read online reviews, which, along with camera advertisements, often provide detailed product information. The next several sections discuss in detail the main points in the preceding list.

Picture Quality

Cameras vary in the quality of images they produce. Picture quality is measured in pixels per inch. As mentioned in Chapter 1, a pixel, short for picture element, is a tiny dot of light that is the basic building block of images on a computer screen or in a digital image. Digital images use millions of pixels to create an image; therefore, most cameras use a megapixel to indicate one million pixels.

The more pixels per inch an image has, the better its picture quality (as shown in Figure 2-4). For example, images generated by a 1.0-megapixel camera have fewer pixels than images generated by a 2.0- or 4.0-megapixel camera.

Figure 2-4 The detail of a digital image depends on the number of pixels per inch it has.

 Keep in mind that new cameras are introduced all the time. Expect to see cameras with even higher pixel ratings in the near future. Also note that a 3-megapixel camera can take pictures at a higher resolution than most computer monitors can display.

File Formats

Some cameras enable you to save your pictures in different formats, which can come in handy depending on how you plan to use your images after you generate them. When you take a picture using a digital camera, the image is saved to a file, which you can then copy to your computer. Depending on the camera, you may have a choice of file formats in which to save the file. The most common file format for digital photos is JPEG (Joint Photographic Experts Group). JPEG is among the most popular formats, not only for printed pictures, but also for pictures displayed on Web pages.

You may also be able to save images as TIFF (Tagged Image File Format) files, which is another popular type. These are often used for printed publications, such as the pictures in this book.

If you are a novice, you don't have to worry about file formats. On the other hand, if you are a professional photographer or you are working on a project that requires pictures in a particular format, be sure to check out this feature.

Camera Storage

Digital cameras store images in internal memory, on a removable card, or both. Storage is important because it determines how many pictures you can take and whether you need additional storage media.

Determining just how much camera storage you need can be tricky for a couple of reasons. For one, you typically have quality options when you take a picture that determine how much file compression is applied to the image. Remember, compressing an image reduces the file size, but also limits the image quality. You often see the term "Economy" used to indicate the highest compression/lowest quality setting (and smallest file size per image), and "Super Fine" used to indicate the lowest compression/highest quality setting (and largest file size per image). Different camera models use different terminology. With the Gateway camera, for example, you can take basic, normal, and fine images. A finer setting generates a higher quality image, but with less compression, at the price of a larger file size.

Another reason why determining camera storage needs can be tricky is that your camera's overall quality (whether it's a 2-megapixel camera, a 3-megapixel camera, and so on) affects the file size of the images it generates. The higher the quality of the image, the more pixels it has, and therefore the more space you need to store it. Table 2-2 gives you an idea of how camera type and image quality can affect file size.

 Check your camera manual for specific information about the approximate size of the image files your camera generates.

Table 2-2 How Camera Type and Image Quality Affect File Size (based on a 1024×768 image)

CAMERA TYPE	IMAGE TYPE	APPROXIMATE IMAGE SIZE
5-megapixel camera	Super Fine	1600 KB
5-megapixel camera	Economy	340 KB
4-megapixel camera	Super Fine	1002 KB
4-megapixel camera	Economy	278 KB
3-megapixel camera	Super Fine	591 KB
3-megapixel camera	Economy	174 KB

 Remember that you can take pictures with different quality settings. Higher-quality images take up more space in your camera's memory, which means you can take fewer pictures before the camera's memory is full. You can save space by deleting any pictures that you don't want. Also, you can clear the memory and start again by downloading the pictures from the camera to your computer and then erasing the camera's memory.

Storage Media

Depending on the type of camera you have, you may be able to supplement its storage space by buying additional storage media in the form of removable media cards. The two most common types of media cards are CompactFlash (shown in Figure 2-5), xD, SD, and SmartMedia. You can also find cameras that use IBM Microdrives.

Not only does this type of media provide a great deal of storage space, it also allows you to transfer the pictures on the media card to your computer or remove the media card and take it to a print service to have the images printed directly from it. See Chapter 7, "Printing Your Images," for more information on printing.

Removable media cards can store anywhere from 4 MB to 512 MB of image data. Common sizes include 16 MB, 32 MB, and 64 MB.

Figure 2-5 CompactFlash is one type of removable media that is compatible with many digital cameras.

It can be tricky to determine how much storage space your removable media cards should contain. Both camera quality and image quality play a role in determining the size of the image files the camera generates, and the size of these image files dictates how much storage you need. Chances are, your camera's manual has specific information about what type of removable media you can use, as well as approximate storage information. Using the example of the 2-megapixel Gateway camera, Table 2-3 lists the number of images each size media card can store. (This table assumes the resolution of the images is 1600×1200.)

Table 2-3 Number of Images Various Removable Media Cards Can Store

SIZE OF CARD	NUMBER OF SUPER FINE-QUALITY IMAGES	NUMBER OF ECONOMY-QUALITY IMAGES
3-MEGAPIXEL IMAGES		
16 MB	25	84
32 MB	51	171
64 MB	103	342
128 MB	207	684
256 MB	415	1370
4-MEGAPIXEL IMAGES		
16 MB	14	52
32 MB	30	108
64 MB	61	217
128 MB	207	435
256 MB	242	846
5-MEGAPIXEL IMAGES		
16 MB	9	46
32 MB	20	96
64 MB	40	188
128 MB	80	376
256 MB	160	752

Display

One of the neatest features of digital cameras is that they display your pictures on an LCD (Liquid Crystal Display) or similar display immediately after you take them. This feature provides instant gratification—it allows you to see your photo immediately. These screens are usually 1.8 inches, but the size can vary. Some cameras also enable you to use the LCD to zoom in on your pictures.

When you select a camera, look at the display to make sure the view is sharp and large enough that you can get a sense of how the picture will look. If you want to be able to zoom in, make sure the camera has this feature.

More About . . . Display Technology

Lately a new type of display on some digital camera models is competing with the standard LCD display. This new type of monitor uses OLED (Organic Light-Emitting Diode) technology to drastically improve battery life and increase brightness. These displays are light and durable, and they have a wide viewing angle of up to 160 degrees.

Camera Size

The size and dimensions of some digital cameras might surprise you; many aren't shaped quite like their film-based counterparts. The dimensions of cameras vary from model to model. Some are similar to traditional cameras, but others are more square in shape. If you're buying a camera, visit a store and handle it first to make sure you like how it feels in your hand. You might be most comfortable with one that is shaped similar to your own film-based camera. The most comfortable cameras are generally those that have metal bodies and a little extra weight for their size, such as the camera shown in Figure 2-6.

Figure 2-6 The Canon PowerShot S230 is a compact digital camera weighing 6.4 oz. It is about the size of a deck of cards.

Camera Features

When you are comparing digital cameras, be sure to find out what type of lens and flash each one uses, as well as what other features are offered. In certain respects, comparing digital cameras is similar to comparing their film-based counterparts. For example, when you look at a digital camera, ask what type of lens it has. Is it fixed or can it be zoomed? If it's a zoom lens, what is the zoom range? Another important question to ask is what type of flash the camera has—automatic, manual, or both. Also, does the camera have automatic red-eye reduction?

More About . . . Lenses

When you compare digital cameras, you will see two types of zoom ranges cited—optical zoom and digital zoom. Optical zoom is the same type of zoom found on regular cameras. With an optical zoom, you actually change the range of space captured by the image sensor. Digital zoom, however, is actually a trick. This type of zoom photographs an entire scene but saves only a particular part or expands a section by adding pixels. You can get the same effect by cropping the image in an imaging program.

Unlike film-based cameras, some digital cameras can also be used for audio/video recording. However, keep in mind that a digital camera isn't going to replace your video camera. You can shoot short videos and capture pictures from the video to use as prints, but you won't get the full features of a video recorder in a camera. Also, digital videos are incredibly large. Most likely, you will be able to shoot only a short film.

Power Source

Most cameras use rechargeable batteries, and they may include a power adapter (sometimes as an optional add-on). Many also come equipped to use AA or other readily available alkaline batteries. Digital cameras use up batteries quickly, and it might be more cost effective to invest in some rechargeable removable batteries or a special heavy-duty battery that attaches to the camera, such as Quantum's QB1 Compact. This type of battery is rechargeable, made just for digital cameras with a power adapter, and lasts for hours or even days, depending on use. When you shop for your camera, you may want to check to see whether it has a port or adapter for such a power source.

Software

Most cameras come with a driver (a file that tells Windows the particular details about the device). In addition, many cameras come with software that downloads images from the camera to the computer and enables you to edit and print the images. Popular software programs include Adobe® Photoshop® Elements and Microsoft Picture It!®. You can find more information about software in the "Selecting an Image Editor" section.

Accessories

In addition to the camera, you might want to consider buying some optional equipment. For example, as with a film-based camera, you might decide you need a carrying case, a tripod, extra batteries, and a power adapter for your digital camera. There are also special accessories for digital cameras, such as the items described in the following list.

+ Some Kodak cameras have a docking station that you can attach to your computer to make transferring images from the camera to the computer easier. The docking station isn't required, but it does simplify the transfer of images.

+ Instead of docking stations, some cameras have a memory-card reader that you can attach to your computer. You can use this reader to transfer images from your removable media card.

+ Special photo printers enable you to print your digital images on paper that looks and feels like regular photographic paper. See the "Printing Your Images" section later in this chapter for an overview of printing choices, and see Chapter 7 for detailed information about printing.

Scanner Basics

Chances are, you have some favorite photos you've taken with your film-based camera. Using a scanner, you can easily convert those photos to digital images and save them as files on your computer. Then you can work with them just like the images you capture using your digital camera. For example, you can scan a photograph taken with a film-based camera at your family reunion and e-mail it to all your family members. Or, you can use your image-editing software to correct flaws (such as red-eye, tears, or stains) in your photo prints. This section covers the basics of using a scanner and the software that comes with it, as well as how to use a scanning service for the same results.

 The specific steps for using your scanner will depend on the make and model of the scanner and the software you use with it. Check your scanner's manual for detailed instructions.

Taking Advantage of Scanning Technology

You already know that you can use a scanner to convert photo prints or negatives into digital files that you can edit, insert into a document, e-mail to friends and family, add to Web pages, organize on your computer, print... the list goes on. However, you can do more with scanners than just convert photographs into digital images. Suppose you're working on a user manual for the nifty invention you've designed. You can use your scanner to convert hand-drawn line art into digital images that you can place in the manual. Or maybe your child drew a picture that you want to share with his grandparents; your scanner will convert that drawing to a digital file that you can drop into an e-mail message.

 You can attach an adapter to some scanners that enables you to scan negatives and slides, as well as paper documents and regular photos. Some scanners, including the Epson Perfection 1250 Photo scanner, can scan both photographic prints and negatives; others can even scan slides.

Scanners are also useful for digitizing important paper documents such as bank, financial, and investment statements; receipts; tax information, and so on. This allows you to store copies of these important documents digitally on your computer, rather than (or in addition to) storing paper copies of them.

 If you need to keep track of numerous contacts in the course of doing business, you might consider purchasing a business-card scanner to scan your contacts' business cards. You can store the information from the card (the contact name, company, phone number, and so on) in a contact-management program on your computer.

If you have fax software, you can even use your scanner to help fax documents from your computer. For example, suppose you need to fax a signed contract to someone. You can sign the contract, scan it, and then fax the digital file from your machine. Alternatively, you can attach the scanned file as an e-mail attachment.

 To fax a file from your machine, you need a fax modem and fax program. Windows XP includes a fax program, but you can purchase separate faxing programs as well.

Types of Scanners

There are several types of scanners, including:

✦ **Flatbed.** The most common type of scanner is a flatbed scanner, which looks and works much like a copy machine. You place the image you want to scan on the transparent glass and close the lid. The scanner then scans the document using a moving light source, converts the image into digital format, and displays the image on the screen.

 When you use a flatbed scanner to scan transparent images, such as slides and negatives, the resulting image will sometimes appear to have concentric circles or rings on it that resemble a giant fingerprint. These are called Newton Rings, and they are a common problem when you are scanning transparent film media. If you are planning to buy a flatbed scanner that handles both pictures and transparent media, ask whether this is a problem for your scanner of choice. Most manufacturers have tried to solve this problem on their newer scanners.

- **Handheld.** Another common type of scanner is a handheld scanner. This sometimes looks similar to a pen, and it is most commonly used to scan text into a computer. You drag the handheld unit across the text you want to scan.

- **Film.** A film scanner is used to scan negatives and slides. You might consider buying a film scanner as you develop your digital-photography skills.

- **Sheet feed.** A sheet feed scanner is most commonly used for reflective material such as transparencies.

 Most scanners have the capability to scan in both color and black-and-white. However, if you plan to scan color photos, be sure to choose a scanner that supports color scanning.

Image Quality

Like digital cameras, scanners vary in the quality of the images they produce. The resolution of a scanner indicates the quality, measured in pixels per inch, or ppi. As with cameras, the higher the resolution, the finer the detail in the scanned image. Generally, 300 ppi is adequate resolution for most users, but high-end scanners can produce scanned images with resolutions as high as 4000 ppi. You might need a higher quality scanner if you are doing professional artwork, detailed architectural prints, or other high-quality printed materials (for instance, a catalog).

> **More About... Image Quality**
>
> Another factor in image quality is color bit depth. A bit is the smallest unit of data that a computer can recognize. Color information is stored in bits—the more bits, the better the range of colors the scanner can read and represent.

Scanner Features

When you shop for a scanner, you first select the type of scanner you want (typically flatbed for pictures). You then find one that can generate the level of quality you need for your scanned images. Once you make these two major decisions, you can start to compare the different features between scanners.

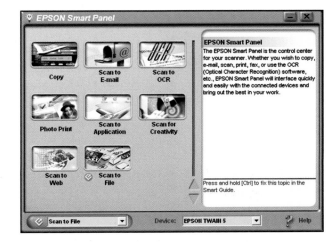

- ✦ **Scanning area.** This determines the size of the document you can scan. Most home and office flatbed scanners have legal-size scanning areas.

- ✦ **Scanning software.** Typically, scanners come bundled with software to handle the image once you've scanned it to your computer.

- ✦ **Connection type.** Scanners are attached to newer computers via a USB port. If you have an older computer, you can connect your scanner using one of the other ports, such as the serial port, or you might consider adding a USB port to your computer. This is a relatively inexpensive and easy upgrade.

Selecting an Image Editor

To manipulate the appearance of images you capture with your camera or scanner, you need some type of image-editing software. Image-editing software enables you to display, print, save, and edit the image.

Here's some good news: Most cameras and scanners come bundled with their own software. For instance, if you buy an Epson scanner, it comes with a scanner program called ArcSoft PhotoImpression. You can use this program to view, edit, and save the scanned image. Likewise, Kodak cameras come with Kodak Picture Software, used to download images from the camera to the computer, as well as to manipulate and save the pictures. Some companies, such as Gateway, bundle everything you need into one package. For example, if you purchase a Photo Solution, you may receive a camera, a software program, and extras such as guides and photo paper.

If your camera or scanner didn't come with its own software, or if you find the software doesn't quite suit your needs, you can always purchase image-editing software on your own. Popular image programs include Microsoft Picture It! and Adobe Photoshop Elements.

 You'll learn more about using Picture It! and Adobe Photoshop Elements in Chapter 5, "Editing and Manipulating Your Images."

All image-editing programs enable you to open, view, print, and save your images, and most enable you to perform the same set of basic editing tasks, including cropping, rotating, annotating, adjusting color, fixing red-eye, and so on. However, the programs differ somewhat in their look and feel, or interface. For example, compare Figure 2-7, showing Photoshop Elements, with Figure 2-8, showing Picture It!.

Figure 2-7 Photoshop Elements is one example of an image-editing program.

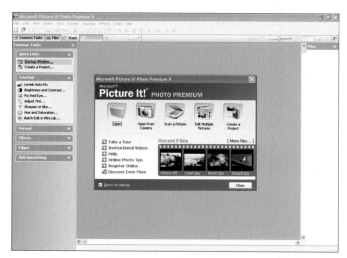

Figure 2-8 Picture It! is another image editor.

The program you choose depends on your preference. If your camera, scanner, or bundle came with its own software, most likely it will work well for you. As you become more experienced, you might want to consider some of the higher-end programs, such as Adobe Photoshop (which is the more advanced, professional version of Adobe Photoshop Elements).

Printing Your Images

All your glorious pictures aren't much use if you can't show them off! Of course, one of the major advantages of digital photography is that you can include images in a document or Web page and send them via e-mail (covered in Chapter 8), but a brag book full of prints can't be beat. Fortunately, there are several printer options to choose from and a number of ways to convert your images to beautiful prints. In this section, you'll learn about a variety of printer features and what to consider if you plan to purchase a printer, as well as other methods you can use to create quality prints.

 For specific details on printing your pictures, see Chapter 7.

Printing Images at Home

There are many brands and styles of printers that allow you to create prints from home. With the large number of options, it is important to look for one that does everything you need—without the additional pricy features you'll never use.

Here are some questions to ask yourself before you purchase a printer:

+ **What type of printer do I want?** These days, the two most common types of printers are inkjet and laser. Inkjet printers spray a fine, quick-drying ink onto paper. Laser printers, on the other hand, work more like copy machines. A laser beam burns special toner on the page to create the image. Inkjet printers are a popular choice because they are quiet and relatively inexpensive, especially if you want a color printer. In addition to inkjet and laser printers, special photo printers are available. These create print-shop-quality prints on regular photo paper. You'll learn more about this special type of printer in Chapter 7.

Several combination printer-copier-fax-scanner machines are now on the market. If you need an office machine that can perform multiple functions, check these out.

✦ **Do I need color?** If you plan to print photographs, you most likely will want a color printer. The most affordable are color inkjet printers, although color laser printers have become more reasonable as color printing has become more popular.

✦ **What level of quality do I need?** A printer's quality is determined by its resolution. For printers, resolution is measured in dots per inch, or dpi. Again, a higher number means a higher-quality printer.

> ### More About . . . Comparing Print Quality
>
> When comparing print quality, you'll usually see resolution listed as something like 1200×1600 dpi. These two figures are the horizontal and vertical dots per inch, respectively. For example, you can expect to find printers with resolutions from 1200×600 dpi to 2400×1200 dpi and up. You might find it difficult, however, to translate such measurements into real results. If you are shopping for a printer, visit some retail stores and compare the printouts from various printers so you can see the difference.

✦ **How fast do I need my printer to be?** Printer speed is measured by the number of pages printed per minute (ppm). Laser printers are usually faster than inkjet printers. For both types of printers, you can expect to find speeds of four to 16 ppm.

Black-and-white printing is faster than color printing, so when you compare printers, you should check both the black-and-white speed and the color speed.

✦ **What type of connection do I need?** Printers commonly connect to computers via the parallel port, also called the LPT (Line Printer) port. Some, however, connect via a serial or USB port. If you have just one printer, you likely have an available port. If you are adding a second printer, be sure you have an available port for it.

2

> ## More About . . . Comparing Printer Features
>
> After you've narrowed down your options, there are a number of other printer features you might want to consider before you make your final choice:
>
> ✦ **Can the printer hold more than one kind of paper?** Some printers have multiple trays, enabling you to use one for plain paper and one for envelopes, letterhead, or other special paper. If your printer will be used in an office setting (even if it's a home office), this feature can be quite handy.
>
> ✦ **How is the paper fed into the printer?** Some printers use a tray that you slide into the front, while others use a tray above the printer that feeds from the top down. Some people prefer one method to the other. Test the printers on your short list to make sure it's easy to load the paper. If you are printing on photo paper or labels, be sure you know which way to load the paper. Since you are printing on only one side of the page, the paper must be inserted properly. A good test is to mark an X on a plain piece of paper and then print something. You can tell by the placement of the X which side of the paper the printer uses.
>
> ✦ **Can you print labels and envelopes?** Most printers enable you to print labels, which is handy for mass mailings. You should also be able to easily print an envelope, be it from an extra paper tray or through manual feed.
>
> ✦ **Can you print directly onto a CD?** Some printers, like the Epson Stylus Photo, can print directly onto printable CDs or DVDs. Printers with this capability also usually include software you can use to easily design your own custom CD/DVD covers.
>
> ✦ **What controls does the printer have?** Expect to have an on/off switch as well as a reset button. The printer also should have some clear way to indicate a problem such as paper jams. Look for error lights or messages that clearly indicate the problem.
>
> ✦ **What do the supplies cost?** In addition to paper, you need to replace the ink cartridges for inkjet printers and the toner cartridge for laser printers. Check out the prices of the replacement cartridges that work for each printer model.

Using Film and Scanning Services

If you want the results of digital photography but you don't want to purchase a camera or scanner, you still have other options. For example, many film-development companies, such as Kodak, enable you to store digital versions of your film-based photo prints on CD or on the Web. After your prints are digitized, you can print, e-mail, or modify them using your computer, just as you would if you had used a scanner or digital camera to obtain them.

If you only need to scan images occasionally, you might not want to purchase a scanner. Fortunately, many copy and print stores offer scanners for customer use. In most cases, you can use the same copy or print shop to print pictures, documents, photo calendars, brochures, or any other specialty item that might require a special type of printer. Many film-processing companies now have in-store scanners you can use to scan your photographs and print copies of any size. Check your local drugstore for one of these kiosks; they are an easy and convenient way to create Christmas cards, family photos, wallet-size pictures, or enlargements.

Other Digital Photo Devices

With more and more people carrying cell phones and PDAs with them regularly, it is no wonder digital cameras have started to appear as features on these devices. Why carry a phone and a camera around when you can use the same device to make calls and take pictures? In this section, you'll take a look at a few of these devices and explore some things you can do with them.

 Most cameras built into phones and PDAs are designed to produce lower-resolution images, generally for display on the smaller LCD monitors included with these devices. If you intend to create prints from your digital images, it is best to use a dedicated digital camera designed to produce photo-quality images. With constant advancements in technology, many expect these devices to produce higher-resolution images in the near future.

Camera Phones

Many features available on digital cameras are also offered on some mobile phones, including color LCD monitors, built-in flash, and the ability to record short movies with or without audio. Like with a regular digital camera, you can save images to internal memory or delete them on the spot. In some ways, the combination of these tools offers you more functionality than either device by itself. Specifically, taking a spontaneous photo and sharing it with others has never been easier. Send photos from your phone directly to another phone, or even send images to any e-mail address over the Internet. Although transferring images often requires an additional charge, these features are surprisingly easy to use. As the price of camera phones continues to drop, you can expect to see them become increasingly popular.

 Camera phones have especially caught on in Japan. More than 30 percent of all mobile phones used in Japan have built-in digital cameras.

Digital Cameras and PDAs

Personal Digital Assistants (PDAs) are getting more advanced all the time. In addition to their original functions related to organizing our complicated lives, these tools can offer built-in mobile phones, digital jukeboxes, Internet access—and yes, integrated digital cameras. Whether they are built into the device or offered as an expansion module, digital cameras on PDAs offer many of the same benefits as camera phones. You can take pictures, e-mail them to friends, and transfer them to your computer. With more computing power, PDAs also offer a mobile way to accomplish the following tasks.

- ✦ View images in greater detail with larger LCD monitors than camera phones (or even most digital cameras).

- ✦ Use software on your PDA to edit images and organize them into albums.

- ✦ Beam images to other PDAs using the infrared technology available on many of these devices.

- ✦ Save images to internal memory or a removable media card to transfer them to another portable device or your computer.

More About . . . Hybrid Digital Cameras

You can also use portable hard drives or flash drives, often used to store and play digital audio files (MP3 players), to store large numbers of digital images. Although you might not be able to view the images using one of these devices, it can be a great tool for storage until you transfer them to your computer. As a matter of fact, you can even purchase hybrid devices, such as the Fujifilm FinePix 40i, which is a 2.4-megapixel digital camera that doubles as an MP3 player.

Taking Great Pictures

By now, you've discovered the advantages of digital photography. You've also explored the equipment that makes working with your digital images easy and fun. Now it's time to learn how to use your digital camera to take digital pictures.

In this chapter, you'll explore the various controls and buttons on your digital camera and discover what each one does. You'll also gain an understanding of basic photography principles. Then you'll learn how to take various kinds of photographs using your digital camera, and you'll wrap up the chapter by studying how you can transfer the digital images on your camera to your computer.

Exploring Your Camera's Features

Unless you're an expert, you might view most of the dials, buttons, and other gizmos on your digital camera as mysterious at best. Getting a handle on how these features and settings work will pave the way to using your digital camera to its fullest potential. A number of common features are displayed in Figure 3-1.

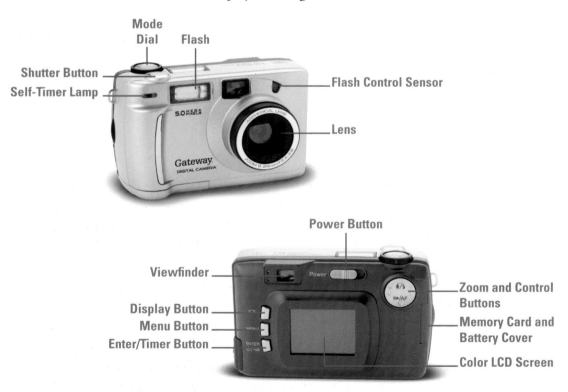

Figure 3-1 Most digital cameras include the features shown here.

Every camera offers different features. Even when two cameras boast the same features, you probably access them in different ways. The best way to determine your camera's features and the best use of them is to read the camera's user manual.

The features that are typically found in digital cameras include the following:

✦ **Lens and lens cover.** The lens and lens cover are easy to locate on the camera's front side. To take pictures, you remove the lens cover or slide it to the side to expose the lens.

✦ **Power button.** To turn on your camera, you need to press the power button, which is typically located either on the side or the top of the camera.

✦ **Connection port.** To transfer pictures from your camera to your computer, connect the cable that came with your camera to your camera's port. The port is usually found on the side of the camera. Refer to Chapter 2 for an illustration of ports and cables for digital cameras and computers.

✦ **Viewfinder.** The viewfinder is a tiny window on the camera's body that you look through to frame your shots. It is generally found on the back of your camera.

✦ **Shutter button.** You press this button, which is almost always located on the top of the camera, to take a picture.

✦ **Flash.** You use a flash to illuminate the subject of your photograph if the setting is too dark.

✦ **Mode dial.** Most digital cameras have several modes—one for taking pictures, another for reviewing or playing back photos, and so on. You use the mode dial, typically found on top of the camera, to switch modes. Figure 3-2 shows a mode dial.

Figure 3-2 Use the mode dial to switch from taking pictures, to recording movies, to reviewing them.

 Many digital cameras also feature a video mode, which allows the camera to shoot short videos in addition to still photos.

✦ **LCD screen.** The LCD screen shows you a preview of a picture you've just taken. You also have the option of switching to playback or review mode, enabling you to view the pictures currently stored on your camera on the LCD screen.

✦ **Menu button.** Many cameras feature a menu button (or something similar) that enables you to access the commands on your camera, such as the Delete command.

✦ **Scroll buttons.** Scroll buttons, which usually look like arrows, enable you to navigate among commands or move from picture to picture.

✦ **Media slot.** If your camera can use a media card such as a SmartMedia, xD, SD, or CompactFlash card, it will have a slot where you insert the card.

✦ **Battery compartment.** One source of a camera's power is supplied by batteries, which are stored in a battery compartment like the one shown in Figure 3-3.

Battery Compartment

SmartMedia Card Slot

Figure 3-3 The door to the battery compartment is usually located on the bottom of the camera.

 In addition to the standard features listed here, your camera may include additional features, such as a strap mount, a tripod mount, or a timer.

Before you can use your camera, you might need to complete a few steps. For specific instructions on completing each of these steps, refer to your camera's user manual.

1 If necessary, insert batteries into the camera's battery compartment. (In some cases, you'll need to charge them first.)

 Many digital cameras come with a rechargeable battery and a power adapter. When the battery is low, you can simply connect the power adapter to the camera to charge the battery. If you need to purchase replacement batteries, be sure to check your digital camera's manual to ensure you purchase batteries compatible with the camera.

2 If your camera uses a media card, insert it into the appropriate slot.

3 You might need to set certain camera options, such as the date and time.

Understanding Basic Photography Principles

As with any new undertaking, one of the very first things you must learn about photography—digital or otherwise—is the terms used by photographers. Learning just a few key photographic terms and concepts will help you decipher your camera's user manual, as well as any articles or how-to information you encounter later.

This section introduces you to some of the key terms and concepts related to digital and film-based photography. You don't need to master all these concepts to begin taking pictures with your digital camera; however, as you become more skilled, you'll appreciate this foundation.

3

Composition

Composition refers to the way you frame the subject of your photograph or compose your image. Use of color, shapes, and lighting are also part of a photo's composition. When composing images, the basic rule is to frame your picture for optimal presentation of its subject. To this end, most beginning photographers frame the subject in the center of the picture. As your photography skills advance, however, you may decide to experiment with other compositions. For example, you might decide to shoot your subject off-center to create a different balance in the picture. Alternatively, you might decide to include more of the background to better show the contrast between your subject and its surroundings. In the photograph shown in Figure 3-4, the photographer has incorporated the landscape to convey the magnitude of the scenery in comparison to the prairie in the foreground.

Figure 3-4 Many factors, including framing, lighting, and color, are part of good composition.

Depth of Field/Focus

When you photograph a subject of any kind, you typically want that person or object to be in focus. Your digital camera uses a lens for focusing, a process that often occurs automatically. With your camera's manual controls, however, you can manipulate your image's depth of field—the area of the photograph that's in focus—by using zoom controls to change the lens's focal length and by adjusting aperture settings.

Zoom Controls

Focal length refers to the distance between the camera's lens and the film or digital sensors the camera uses to record an image. A shorter focal length yields a wider angle of view, meaning that the subject of the photograph will be relatively small in comparison to the background, as shown in Figure 3-5. A longer focal length, on the other hand, yields a narrower angle of view, which means that the subject of the photograph will appear larger in the frame.

Regular Focal Length   **Zoomed Focal Length**

Figure 3-5 A shorter focal length yields a wider angle of view.

If your camera has zoom controls, you can use them to adjust the lens's focal length. In fact, most digital cameras offer multiple zoom settings, usually indicated as 2X (a magnification factor of two) or 3X (a magnification factor of three). The higher the magnification, the closer the subject of the photograph will appear.

 Because digital cameras use smaller lenses than film-based cameras, the focal length and zoom are not the same as those used by 35mm cameras. For instance, the diagonal measurement of a digital frame is approximately 43mm, whereas the normal lens on a 35mm camera is about 50mm. To avoid confusion, most digital cameras give a 35mm equivalent instead of the camera's actual focal length.

Aperture Settings

In automatic mode, your digital camera sets the focus (and, by extension, the depth of field) automatically. In manual mode, however, you can tinker with the depth of field by changing the camera's aperture settings.

A camera's aperture is the opening through which light enters before striking the film or digital sensors. You can increase or decrease the diameter of this opening by changing the aperture settings, also called f-stops. A lower f-stop indicates a greater aperture diameter and vice versa. Figure 3-6 demonstrates how aperture settings can change the appearance of an image. The photo on the left has a small aperture and great field depth, whereas the photo on the right has a large aperture and shallow field depth. Although the two photos appear to be focused differently, the camera was focused on the girl in each.

Figure 3-6 You can adjust the diameter of the aperture to control the depth of field.

Exposure

In photography, be it digital or film-based, you must expose your camera's digital sensors or film to light in order to take a photograph. The term exposure refers to the amount of light allowed to travel through the camera's lens and aperture and strike its digital sensors or film when the shutter is opened.

There are two ways to alter the amount of light that strikes the camera's digital sensors or film. One is to adjust the camera's aperture settings, which increases or decreases the amount of light that can pass through by making the aperture larger or smaller, respectively. The other option is to increase or decrease the camera's shutter speed—that is, the amount of time the shutter remains open. The longer the shutter is open, the more light can pass through. Figure 3-7 demonstrates how exposure can affect the quality of an image.

Overexposed

Underexposed

Proper Exposure

Figure 3-7 An incorrect amount of light allowed to pass through the lens aperture can result in an extra-bright or extra-dim photograph.

 If you want to change your camera's aperture and shutter-speed settings manually, you might need an additional piece of equipment called a light meter to help you avoid overexposing your photograph (using too much light) or underexposing it (using too little light). A light meter measures the levels of light in the scene you want to photograph and enables you to determine the f-stop and shutter speed that will work best. A detailed discussion on using light meters, f-stops, and shutter-speed settings to take photographs is beyond the scope of this book. Fortunately, most digital cameras have built-in meters to handle that job for you.

Rather than make you adjust the aperture and shutter-speed settings manually, most digital cameras have an automatic-exposure mode that determines the best focus, aperture, and shutter speed for each picture. Some digital cameras, however, enable you to fiddle with the automatic-exposure settings. For example, you might adjust an Exposure Compensation setting to change the brightness of the image. This comes in handy when your subject and background brightness vary greatly. In addition, some cameras have special exposure settings for various types of pictures, such as action shots, panoramic shots, portraits, and others. See the "Taking Specialized Photos" section later in this chapter for more information.

Lighting and Flash

As you photograph your subject or scene, be sure to consider lighting. If you're outdoors, the sunlight overhead might be intense and cast shadows on your subject that may not be visually pleasing. If you're indoors, the lighting may be insufficient for correct exposure.

One way to adjust the lighting for your image is to move the subject to a position where the lighting is more pleasing or robust. Alternatively, you can use artificial lighting—be it lighting designed with photography in mind or lighting designed simply to illuminate a room—to enhance available light. Finally, you can use a built-in camera flash to supplement natural or available light.

Using a built-in flash often results in improved color, exposure, and picture sharpness, but it can also wash out your subject, making it blend in with the background. Many digital cameras feature automatic flashes, which are activated whenever the camera detects low-light conditions. In most cases, however, you can also use the camera's menu to adjust the flash settings.

Common flash settings include the following:

✦ **Auto.** Choose this setting if you want your camera to activate the flash when the lighting of the shot requires it. This is usually the default flash setting.

✦ **Red-eye.** When you photograph people in certain conditions (low light, for example), the use of a flash sometimes makes their eyes look red. When you select the red-eye feature, the camera uses a pre-flash, which strobes immediately before you take the picture. This strobe occurs in addition to a regular flash, which strobes the instant the photograph is taken. As a result, red-eye is eliminated. The pre-flash causes the pupils of the subjects' eyes to shrink before the main flash goes off, thus reducing the chance that

the light will reflect off the retinas in the back of the eye, which is the cause of red-eye in photos. See Chapter 5, "Editing and Manipulating Your Images," for details on how to remove red-eye.

✦ **Forced or fill.** Select this option when you want to use the flash regardless of lighting conditions. This is a good choice when you're shooting photographs in fluorescent lighting. This setting will basically relight the scene using the color-corrected light from the flash rather than allowing the lighting from the fluorescent bulb to cast its lovely green glow over your subject. It's also helpful for removing shadows when you shoot in bright light or sunlight.

✦ **Suppressed or off.** Choose this option to disable or suppress the flash regardless of lighting conditions. You might choose this setting if you know that using the flash won't help (for example, when the subject is out of the flash's range) or when you're shooting photos at night and you don't want the entire scene illuminated.

Taking Photographs

Using your digital camera to take photographs is extremely simple—especially if the camera is set to automatic mode. After you've grasped the basics, undoubtedly you'll want to move on to more advanced photographic techniques. In this section, you'll learn how to take basic pictures, and you'll get a few tips and tricks to move you to the next step of digital photography.

Using Automatic Mode

Although the preceding section briefly discussed how you can change camera settings to affect focus, exposure, and flash, most digital cameras can adjust these settings automatically. In automatic mode, you only need to point and shoot to take the picture. You'll find that using your camera's automatic mode works for most pictures and frees you to concentrate on the basics of composing and shooting photographs.

To take a photograph in automatic mode, follow these steps:

 The steps outlined here are general; they may differ somewhat from camera to camera. Read your digital camera's user manual for specific instructions on taking photographs.

❶ Turn the camera on.

❷ Set the camera to automatic mode.

 The Gateway™ DC-T50 features a dial on top with several icons. The "A" icon represents automatic mode; turn the dial to this mode.

❸ Open the lens cover.

If you can't get your camera to display or shoot an image, make sure the lens cover is entirely open. With some cameras, the lens cover must be pushed all the way open until it clicks.

❹ Point your camera at the subject you want to shoot, using the viewfinder or LCD screen to center the subject.

❺ Press the shutter button halfway down to engage the camera's auto-focus feature.

❻ Press the shutter button the rest of the way down to take the picture.

The auto-focus features on most cameras automatically focus on the object or person in the center of the viewfinder. However, you may decide that you want to compose your image differently, perhaps with the subject to one side. Fortunately, many digital cameras offer a workaround. Center the subject in the viewfinder and then push the shutter button down halfway. Doing this locks the focus. Then, offset the viewfinder to one side or the other before taking the shot. Your subject will remain in focus.

❼ Check the LCD screen to preview your image. You can either keep the image or discard it. You'll learn more about discarding images in Chapter 4, "Organizing and Managing Your Images."

Using Zoom Controls

When you're comfortable using your camera in automatic mode, you're ready to start experimenting with other features, such as flash settings or zooming. As mentioned previously, your camera uses zoom controls to change its focal length. A shorter focal length yields a wider angle of view (or zooms out), whereas a longer focal length yields a narrower angle of view (or zooms in).

To get the hang of your camera's zoom features, try the following steps:

The steps outlined here are general; they may differ somewhat from camera to camera. Read your digital camera's user manual for specific instructions on using its zoom feature.

1. Point your camera at the subject and preview the photo using the LCD screen.
2. Press the zoom button. You might see the current zoom settings on the LCD screen.
3. Press the zoom adjustment buttons to change the zoom. Continue pressing the buttons until you're satisfied with the size of your photograph's subject in relation to the background.
4. Reframe your shot, placing your subject in the position you want.
5. Press the shutter button halfway down to use the camera's auto-focus feature to refocus the shot at the new zoom level.
6. Press the shutter button the rest of the way down to take the picture.

Taking Specialized Photos

As you become more adept at using your digital camera, you might want to extend your repertoire from simple snapshots to more specialized images, such as portraits, close-ups, nighttime scenes, or action photos. You can find entire books devoted to each of these subjects. This section briefly outlines a few issues to consider when using a digital camera to capture specialized images. For more on image quality, see Chapter 2.

 The best way to learn to shoot photographs of any kind, whether portraits or action shots, is to experiment. Fortunately, when you use your digital camera, buying film and paying for developing is not a concern!

Shooting Portraits

Whether you're shooting your dog or your Great-Uncle Norm, you'll want to consider the following pointers when you shoot portraits.

 These tips apply whether you're shooting a posed portrait or a candid shot.

✦ **Use lighting to your advantage.** When you're outside, make sure that your subject isn't looking into the sun and that you aren't pointing your camera into the sun. This can cause you to underexpose your subject because the camera will adjust itself to expose for the bright light of the sun. When you're inside, look for soft light, which you can often find by windows. In addition to placing your subject in flattering lighting, you also might want to use a flash.

✦ **Consider your background.** If you want the background to be part of the picture, use something simple. This ensures that the background doesn't detract from your subject.

✦ **Shoot from a good angle.** In most cases, the best angle is eye-level, but you can also get good shots by shooting from a higher point.

 Lower camera levels usually result in unflattering pictures.

✦ **Capture your subject's personality.** As the saying goes, the eyes are the windows to the soul. Focus on eyes to capture your subject's personality. You'll also find that capturing your subject in a relaxed pose improves your portraits.

Close-up Photography

Many small objects, such as flowers, insects, or coins, look best when photographed up close. You also might want to shoot portraits close up to truly capture the details of your subject's face. Regardless of subject, you'll find it easy to shoot close-ups using your digital camera's close-up mode. In this mode, the camera automatically adjusts the focus, flash, and zoom for the best results.

The exact name of the close-up mode varies from camera to camera. For example, Fujifilm FinePix model cameras call this Macro mode, whereas the Kodak calls it Close-up mode. Check your user manual to see whether your camera offers any special modes for taking close-up pictures.

Following are a few things to consider when you shoot close-ups:

+ When photographing small objects close up, consider the background very carefully. It should generally be clean and uncluttered, and it should not draw attention from the subject.

+ If possible, lay a small object flat and photograph it from above. Try standing on a chair if necessary.

+ If portions of the image are out of focus, try backing away from the subject and zooming in on it.

For telephoto images or extreme close-ups, you might consider purchasing an additional lens for your camera. Check with your camera's manufacturer to see what types are available.

Night Photography

Photographing at night presents a unique challenge. If you're photographing a nighttime scene that also features bright lights, your camera will most likely be fooled into thinking there's more light than there actually is, and it will set the aperture, shutter speed, and flash accordingly. The result will be an underexposed, potentially blurry image that leaves much of the scene in the dark.

When photographing at night, try the following tricks:

+ Take a sample picture and preview the results. Then you can make any necessary adjustments to the flash or exposure settings.

✦ If possible, mount the camera on a tripod to prevent movement. Even the tiniest camera movement can make the resulting photograph blurry, especially if the shutter speed has been reduced to accommodate low-light conditions.

Action Photos

Some of the most memorable pictures are those that capture a moment frozen in time—the winning shot in a basketball game, a downhill ski racer hurtling past a gate, a Formula 1 car hugging a hairpin turn. The key to taking action photos is to be ready for that magic moment. Here are a few tips:

✦ Get as close to the action as possible, both physically and by zooming in on it.

✦ Be ready, with your camera to your eye at all times. You never know when a dramatic moment will occur.

✦ Don't shoot just anything. Wait for something exciting to occur, such as a runner sliding into second base or a dolphin breaching from the water.

✦ Some cameras feature a multi-frame mode, which is useful for action photographs because it enables you to take a series of photographs by simply holding down the shutter button. Check your camera's manual for information about using this mode.

✦ As you become a more advanced photographer, read up on the details of shutter speed (faster is better) and f-stops (lower numbers mean a larger aperture and a better action photo).

Shooting Movies

In addition to enabling you to shoot photographs, many cameras also have a movie mode, which you can use to make short videos (20 seconds or longer, depending on the amount of memory in your camera). To shoot a movie using your digital camera, follow these steps:

1 Switch your camera to movie mode.

 On the Gateway CD-T50 camera, movie mode is designated on the mode dial by the icon that looks like a movie camera.

2 Press the shutter button and release it to start shooting the movie. You should see **REC** displayed on the LCD screen.

3 When you've finished shooting the movie, press the shutter button a second time.

 Windows XP includes a movie-editing program called Windows Movie Maker, which you can use to edit your movies.

After you've shot your movie, you can preview it in Preview mode and transfer it to your computer, just as you would a still photograph. You'll learn more about previewing and transferring images and movies in the next chapter.

 Many cameras include a built-in microphone that captures audio while recording movies. Some also include a speaker that allows you to listen to the audio you have recorded while previewing your movies. Consult your camera's manual for details regarding audio recording and playback.

Improving Your Picture-Taking Skills

In addition to the specific situations I mentioned, there are a number of other tricks that can help you improve the quality of your photographs. Without delving too deeply into advanced techniques, in this section you'll learn some quick ways to create better-looking photographs.

Focal Point and Framing

Be sure to choose the main point of interest when you take a photograph. Although a picture may be filled with many interesting things, it's always best to select a single subject. When you have found your subject, it is called the focal point. The focal point is not necessarily at the center of the photograph. Placing the focal point to the side, for example, can offer a more interesting composition.

Also, as you establish the subject and prepare to take a photograph, be sure to observe the boundaries in the viewfinder. The human eye sometimes misses objects in the peripheral portion of a scene, and you might be surprised to see the detail lurking at the fringes of your photograph. While taking a picture, aim to draw the viewer to the focal point by placing less-pronounced elements at the edge of the viewfinder.

 Sometimes the viewfinder can distort the boundaries when you are shooting close-up photography. In that case, try using the camera's LCD display as a viewfinder for an accurate presentation before taking the shot.

The Rule of Thirds

The Rule of Thirds is one method a photographer might employ to capture a pleasing composition. To use the Rule of Thirds in your own photography, imagine two evenly spaced horizontal and vertical lines through your image as you look through the viewfinder. Then, instead of placing the subject in the center of the photograph, adjust the viewfinder so that the subject runs into one of these imaginary lines. You might also treat these lines as boundaries. In Figure 3-8, for example, basic elements of this landscape are distributed according to this grid.

Figure 3-8 Professional photographers sometimes use a grid based on the Rule of Thirds to produce a balanced photograph.

The Rule of Thirds technique derives from the ancient Greek concept of the Golden Rectangle, which is basically the same shape as a normal photograph today. Artists and photographers have found that images split evenly into nine smaller rectangles tend to give balance and order to a composition.

To aid you in this, some digital cameras actually overlay a grid pattern on the LCD screen or in your viewfinder, as is the case with the Fujifilm FinePix 2650Zoom camera's Framing Guideline feature. (To access this feature on the FinePix 2650Zoom, press the DISP button until the Framing Guideline option appears.) Check your camera's manual to see whether it has a similar feature.

Other Tips and Tricks

Here are some other things to consider while taking photographs with your digital camera:

- ✦ Keep the camera steady while you are taking photos. In other words, limit your movement as much as possible while the shutter is open. Particularly in nighttime photos, you might consider placing the camera on a platform. Although a tripod is perhaps the best choice, setting your camera on a rock or post can work just as well.

 You will find a threaded mount on the bottom of most digital cameras that is used to affix the camera to a tripod. On consumer-model cameras, this mount is almost always one-quarter inch in diameter, which is compatible with most available tripods.

- ✦ Use the flash during the daytime to eliminate dark shadows cast by the bright sun. Most cameras include a Force Flash setting that allows you to use the flash regardless of the lighting conditions.

- ✦ Don't be afraid to take test shots. Try different angles, zoom in, use the flash, and so on, and then view the results on the camera's display. You don't have to worry about film; just delete the images you don't want to keep.

- ✦ Use both orientations. A picture taken in the standard horizontal orientation tends to create an illusion of broadness, whereas a vertically aligned image can give the impression of height. Generally, scenes lend themselves to one of these two orientations. For example, scenes with horizontal lines, especially those with a horizon, are usually better suited for the standard horizontal format. Tall structures such as buildings or monuments often are well suited for a vertical format.

◆ Use both viewfinders. Remember, if you can't get the angle you want using the traditional viewfinder, you can use the LCD display.

 Some digital cameras, such as the Canon PowerShot G3, feature a flip-out display that swivels so you can turn the camera around to photograph yourself while previewing the image.

◆ Try stepping back and zooming in. In addition to using your camera's macro setting to take a picture just inches from your subject, you can move back a bit and use the camera's zoom controls. This technique can alleviate the problems with distorted backgrounds that are inherent with close-ups, and it may produce a more desirable image.

3

Organizing and Managing Your Images

M any people use a photo album to organize and protect their printed photographs. You might have one of your own. In fact, depending on how many photos you have, you might have several albums. Each album may represent a year in your life, or you might have albums containing photos from a single significant event, such as your wedding or your trip to Hawaii.

Just as you organize your print photos in albums, you likely need some way to organize and protect the digital images stored on your computer. That way, you won't waste time looking all over your hard drive for a particular image. In fact, you can even group related photos in virtual albums that act much like their real-world counterparts by using specialized image-management software. As an added bonus, you can create slideshows of those pictures to show to your friends. You might also decide to store your digital images on other media, such as CDs or Zip disks, either to free space on your hard drive or to have backup files in the event that something happens to the files on your machine. In this chapter, you'll learn how to do all that and more.

 The steps outlined throughout this chapter are general ones. As you read through steps outlined in this chapter, you might find that buttons and menus are named differently on your digital camera. If you are having trouble finding the corresponding button or menu on your camera, consult your camera's user manual.

Using Your Digital Camera to Manage Photographs

Unlike film-based photographs, which must be developed and printed either by you or a photo lab before they can be seen, digital photos are available for viewing instantly. Added to this convenience is the fact that if an image isn't up to par, you can delete it from your camera's memory right away—no messy chemicals or hefty processing fees required. When your camera or removable media device finally runs out of memory, you can transfer the digital images you choose to save to your computer, which you can then use to store, manipulate, print, and e-mail your photos.

> ### More About . . . Tracking Available Memory
>
> Unlike a roll of film, which allows you to take only a set number of photographs (typically 12, 24, or 36), the number of photos you can store in your camera's memory or removable media device depends on how much memory you started with, as well as the image quality of the photographs you take. Fortunately, many cameras calculate how many more photos will fit in memory and display this information on the LCD screen. In addition, most cameras display an error message when they've run out of memory.

In this section, you'll learn how to preview and discard images, as well as how to transfer images to your computer.

 Take as many pictures as you want with your digital camera! Because you can discard the ones that don't turn out well before they're ever printed, you don't have to worry about wasting film.

Previewing Photographs

With most digital cameras, you use one mode to take photos and another—typically called Playback or Preview—to preview them on your camera's LCD screen. In this mode, you can scroll through all the pictures you've taken. To preview your images, follow these steps:

Playback Mode

❶ Switch your camera to **Playback** mode.

 The name of this mode varies by camera. Read your camera's user guide to determine which mode is used for deleting photos.

❷ Press the **Back** and **Forward** buttons to scroll through your pictures.

 Some cameras enable you to magnify a picture to view it in more detail. Most can also display several photographs at once so you can easily navigate to a specific shot. The zoom controls are often used for these functions when the camera is in Playback mode. Check your camera's user manual for information about using these features.

Deleting Photographs

No doubt you'll take a photo that doesn't turn out as you expected, especially when you're getting used to using your new digital camera. Not to worry! You can delete any pictures you don't want, thereby freeing up space on your camera or removable media device for pictures that make the grade.

To delete images from your camera, follow these steps:

❶ Change to **Playback** mode.

❷ Scroll through your photos until the one you want to delete is displayed.

❸ Press the **Menu** button.

 This button lets you scroll through and select different commands, including the command for deleting pictures. If your camera has a dedicated Delete button (which might look like a trash can), simply press that button to delete the current photo.

❹ Using the camera's arrow buttons, scroll to the Erase command (or a command with a similar name, such as Delete).

 If you want to delete all the photos currently stored in your camera's memory, use the camera's menu to locate a command named Erase All Frames, Delete All, or something similar.

❺ Press the **Select** button to select the command.

❻ To confirm the deletion, use your camera's arrow keys to select **OK** or **Yes**.

Understanding Digital File Formats

As you discovered in Chapter 2, your digital camera most likely stores its images in JPEG format. After you transfer these files to your computer, you can copy, move, rename, or delete them like other file types. Virtually all image-editing software can open JPEG images, and most are capable of saving your JPEG images to TIFF or other file formats. Simply open the JPEG file in the image-editing program, and then choose Save As from the File menu. You can choose to save the image in a variety of different formats. You'll learn more about image-editing software in Chapter 5, "Editing and Manipulating Your Images."

Following is a list of common digital image formats and how they are most often used:

✦ **JPEG (Joint Photographic Experts Group).** Used by most digital cameras for storage, JPEGs can have up to 16.8 million colors. Although some information is lost to preserve a small file size, you can lower compression settings to achieve higher quality.

✦ **TIFF (Tagged Image File Format).** Although graphics in this format are generally larger than JPEG files, they can offer very high-quality images and they are capable of 16.8 million colors. This format is commonly used for image editing and publication.

 Some high-end digital cameras can store photos in TIFF format.

✦ **GIF (Graphics Interchange Format).** Because of their small size and features such as animation, GIF graphics are often used for Web pages. However, because they are limited to 256 different colors, they are not the best choice for photographs.

✦ **EXIF (Extended File Format).** Digital cameras use this format to store additional information along with the image data, such as the date, time, or whether the flash was used. This data can be useful when you're editing an image. Figure 4-1 shows EXIF data accessed from Adobe Photoshop Elements.

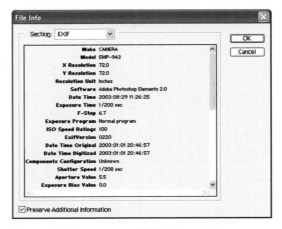

Figure 4-1 You can use EXIF data, which accompanies digital photos taken with most digital cameras, for reference while editing the image.

✦ **BMP (Microsoft Bitmap Format).** This is the format used for Microsoft Paint. BMP files can be up to 16.8 million colors, but they are larger than JPEG files.

✦ **PDF (Portable Document Format).** You can open files in PDF format for onscreen display using Adobe's Acrobat Reader, which is offered as a free download from Adobe (http://www.adobe.com/products/acrobat/readermain.html). Because of their small size and versatility, PDF files are often used for Web pages and transfer over the Internet. They can only be saved using one of Adobe's products, such as Photoshop Elements or Photoshop Album.

 Because PDF files can be created from Adobe's image-editing, illustration, or page-layout software, electronic documents of all types are commonly found in PDF format. You can also optimize PDF files for printing.

✦ **PSD (Photoshop Format).** This is the native format of Adobe Photoshop and Adobe Photoshop Elements. Unlike generic formats, such as TIFF or JPEG, image-editing data (such as layers and selections) is saved with PSD files. You can open files saved in this format in Photoshop products. Some other image-editing programs are also capable of opening PSD files.

Now that you've learned the basics and available formats for managing your photographs, it's time to actually get those photos onto your computer so you can explore the full potential of digital images.

Transferring Images to Your Computer

After you've taken a series of photos and deleted the ones you don't want, you can transfer the remaining photos to your computer. In addition to enabling you to store, manipulate, print, and e-mail your photos, transferring photos from your camera has the added benefit of allowing you to free up space so you can store additional photos in your camera's memory or removable media device.

Before you can transfer your photos to your computer, however, you must set it up to handle this operation. In this section, you'll learn how to configure your computer and camera for easy transfer and how to use Windows XP to perform the transfer operation. In this section, you will also learn how to set up a scanner and import scanned images.

Setting Up Your Computer

Before you can transfer digital images to your computer, you must install the camera or scanner on your computer, just as you would a printer or any other hardware device. The installation process copies the drivers your computer needs to communicate with your camera.

The first step to installing your camera or scanner is to connect it (or removable media) to the appropriate port on your computer using the connection cable that came bundled with the camera or scanner. (You might need to pull back a cover to reveal the camera's connection port.)

 Most cameras or camera media connect to computers via a USB (Universal Serial Bus) or FireWire port. Sometimes these ports are found on the front of the computer, but some computers have USB and/or FireWire ports on the back or the back and front. If your port is on the back, it should be right below the cables for the mouse and the keyboard. For more information about cameras and ports, refer to Chapter 2.

After you've connected your camera or scanner to your computer, you'll use one of two methods to install it—plug-and-play setup or manual setup. The process which you use will depend largely on the type of digital camera or scanner you have and the version of Windows you have on your computer.

 Try installing your camera or scanner via plug-and-play first. If that doesn't work, use one of the manual methods.

Plug-and-Play Setup

In many cases, Windows can recognize when a new component is added to your system and install it automatically. This is called plug-and-play setup. In this scenario, Windows queries the new device to find out details about it and then searches the driver files that were installed with the operating system for the one needed to communicate with that device. If Windows locates the driver file, it installs it on your system.

To use plug-and-play setup, you simply connect your camera, camera media, or scanner to your computer. If plug-and-play setup is successful, a message will appear in the notification area on the Taskbar, indicating that the hardware (in this case, your camera) was found and installed properly.

Manual Setup

Unfortunately, Windows doesn't always have the driver file you need to install a new component. In that case, you'll need to install the device manually. To do so, insert the CD-ROM or floppy disk that came with your camera or scanner in the appropriate drive on your computer. In most cases, a manual setup routine will start automatically and walk you through the installation process. Simply follow the instructions that appear on your screen.

If the setup routine doesn't start automatically, you can still use the CD-ROM to install the driver with the help of the Microsoft Scanner and Camera Wizard.

 All steps in this chapter assume you have Windows XP installed on your computer.

❶ Choose **Control Panel** from the **start** menu. The Control Panel opens.

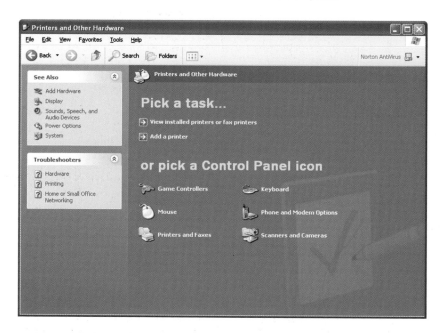

❷ Click on **Printers and Other Hardware**. The Printers and Other Hardware window opens.

❸ Under Pick a Control Panel, click **Scanners and Cameras**. The Scanners and Cameras window opens, displaying any scanners or digital cameras currently installed on your computer.

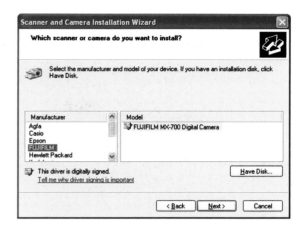

4 In the Task list, click **Add an imaging device**. The Welcome screen of the Microsoft Scanner and Camera Wizard appears.

5 Click **Next**. The second screen of the Wizard appears.

6 Insert the disc that came with the camera or scanner in the appropriate drive and click **Have Disk**. The Install From Disk screen appears.

 If you prefer, you can also see whether Windows has a driver that will work for your camera or scanner. To do this, select its manufacturer from the list on the left side of the screen and the model from the list on the right. Click **Next** and follow any instructions for installing a driver from the drivers that come pre-installed with Windows.

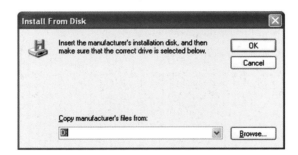

7 Select the **Copy manufacturer's files from** drop-down menu and click the drive containing the disc. Then click **Browse**. The Locate File dialog box will appear.

8 Select the driver file from the drive you specified in the preceding step and click **Open**.

9 Click **Finish**. Windows installs the appropriate driver for your camera or scanner.

 If your camera or scanner didn't come with a CD or floppy disk, or if the CD or disk doesn't contain the driver file you need, check your camera manufacturer's website. Manufacturers commonly post updated driver files you can download and install on your computer. To download the driver, follow the specific instructions on your manufacturer's site. After the driver has been downloaded to your computer, note where it's stored and then select this location after you click on Have Disk in Step 6.

Once your computer has the correct driver installed, you're ready to transfer pictures from your camera or scan images, documents, pictures, or illustrations with your scanner. As mentioned previously, you can transfer photos easily using Windows XP. You'll learn how in the next section.

 Some cameras and scanners require you to use their own transfer and editing programs, which are typically launched when you attach the camera or camera media to your computer. Even if your device requires you to use its own software, most likely you'll be able to use the Microsoft Scanner and Camera Wizard to transfer pictures. Photoshop Elements, Photoshop Album, and even Microsoft Word have options for importing images directly from a scanner or camera.

Importing Images from Your Camera

Microsoft Scanner and Camera Wizard leads you through the process of downloading images from your camera to your computer. Simply follow these steps:

1 Connect the camera or camera media to the appropriate port on your computer and, if necessary, turn on the camera.

2 When you are prompted by the Removable Disk dialog box, select **Copy pictures to a folder on my computer using Microsoft Scanner and Camera Wizard**, and then click **OK**.

 If you are not prompted by the Removable Disk dialog box, click the **start** button and select **My Computer**. If the camera is properly connected to the computer, you will see an icon labeled Removable Disk. Double-click **Removable Disk**, and open any folders therein until you see your image files. Then, you can drag them to another folder, such as My Pictures, to copy them to your hard drive as you would any other file. Or, select the images, and then in the Task pane on the left, under File and Folder Tasks, choose **Copy the selected items**. Then choose the destination folder and click **OK**.

❸ Windows will read the camera or removable media and then display the Wizard's Welcome screen. Click **Next**.

❹ The Wizard will display thumbnail versions of each picture stored on the camera or camera media. By default, all the images are selected. To prevent Windows from downloading an image, click it to cancel the selection. Alternatively, you can click **Clear All** to clear all image selections, and then click the images you want. After you have selected the images you want to transfer, click **Next**.

❺ By default, Windows places all the selected images in a folder within the My Pictures folder, which is located in the My Documents folder. To specify a name for this folder, type it in the text box labeled **1. Type a name for this group of pictures**, or select a name from the drop-down menu.

 Every Windows XP user has a unique My Pictures folder that is the default location for storing images.

❻ To specify a different location for the new folder, click **Browse** and navigate to the drive and folder where you want the new folder containing your pictures to be stored.

❼ To delete the pictures from your camera after they've been copied to your computer, click **Delete pictures from my device after copying them**.

 It's a good idea to delete the photos from your camera after you've transferred them because it frees up space for any new photos you take. However, the first few times you transfer pictures, you might want to leave them on the camera just to make sure the transfer went through without a hitch. After you've verified that the images were successfully transferred, you can use the commands in your camera's menu to delete the images from the camera's memory.

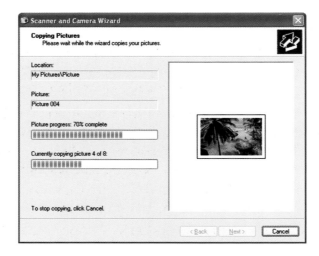

8. Click **Next**. The images will be copied to the folder you've specified.
9. Now you'll be prompted to select what you want to do next. You can publish the pictures to a Web site, order prints online, or do nothing.
10. Click **Nothing. I'm finished working with these pictures**, and then select **Next**.
11. Click **Finish** to close the Wizard. After you have transferred the images to your computer, you can open the folder they're stored in and review, modify, or print them.

Now that you have downloaded your images to your computer, you are ready to enhance and print them. Chapter 5 covers opening and modifying pictures, and Chapter 7, "Printing Your Images," outlines the procedure for printing them.

However, you don't have to have a digital camera to transfer images to your computer. You can also use a scanner to capture existing photographs and send them to your computer. The following sections explain how to set up your scanner and transfer traditional prints to your computer as digital image files.

Scanning Existing Photographs

Transferring scanned images to your computer works much the same way as transferring images with a digital camera. A scanner basically takes a high-resolution picture of a photograph and sends the image data to your computer. Once the image file is on your computer, you can copy, delete, or manipulate it just like images transferred from your digital camera.

Scanning an Image

Your scanner works much like a copy machine. You place the image you want to scan on the scanner's bed, and then you scan it. The scanner copies the image data, converts it to digital information, and displays it on your computer in the scanner's software program.

The specific steps for scanning—such as the commands to select and the range of scanning options—vary across scanner models, but the basic steps are essentially the same. The following list illustrates the general steps for a flatbed scanner. For specific information, check the manual for your particular scanner and scanner software.

1 Click on **start**, **All Programs**, and then point to the scanner program folder and select the program. Alternatively, you can scan from another program.

 In Adobe Photoshop Elements, for example, you can click the **File** menu and choose **Import** and then your scanner device to access Photoshop Album's scanning utility. If you use this method, the scanned photo opens directly in Photoshop Elements.

2 When the scanning program window opens, place the image you want to scan facedown in the top corner of the scanner's view area. (Check your scanner manual to find out exactly where to place the image. Like copiers, scanners usually indicate the start area with an arrow and include paper dimensions.) Close the scanner lid.

3 Set any available scanning options. For instance, you might be able to select the purpose for which the scanned document will be used (such as editing text, faxing, filing, or copying) and the type of image (black and white, color, and so on). You can also select mode (color, grayscale, or black and white), resolution, size, and other options. These options vary depending on the scanner. In Office XP's scanning program, you can select the color, (black and white, black and white from color page, color, or grayscale) as well as options for the paper (whether it is double-sided, for instance).

❹ Some programs display a preview of the scan automatically. Others, such as Adobe Photoshop Album's scanning utility (shown in Figure 4-2), require you to click on a preview button to preview the scan.

❺ Click on the menu command or button to start the scan. Most programs include a menu command such as File, Acquire, as well as a toolbar shortcut. Check with your program for the particular command to start the scan. In Photoshop Album, you click **Scan**.

Figure 4-2 Photoshop Album's ScanGear CS window displays a preview of the image before you scan to a file.

Working with Scanned Images

After you have scanned an image, you can manipulate it using your scanner program. Although every scanner program is different, most enable you to edit the image in several ways. The following list details some common image-editing options:

✦ **Cropping the image.** Save just the portion of the image you want and remove the rest.

✦ **Erasing part of the image.** Drag over any parts of the image you want to erase.

✦ **Annotating the image.** Add notes to the image to call out points of interest. Alternatively, add text or freehand drawings to the image.

✦ **Flipping or rotating the image.** Rotate the image left or right. Many programs enable you to select the exact degree of rotation.

✦ **Adjusting colors, brightness, and contrast.** Fine-tune these settings to improve the image, or distort the colors for effect.

✦ **Zooming around the image.** Zoom in or out for close editing work.

✦ **Printing the image.** Print a hardcopy of the image.

✦ **Saving the image.** Specify the image's file type, location, and quality.

Because many scanner programs use a generic name for the scan (often the date), it's a good idea to resave the image using a more descriptive name. For example, "Mosaic Peace Stone" is more descriptive than "Monday, September 1, 2003." Doing so will help you identify the file later.

You can open an image in your scanner program and use the program tools (such as the toolbar buttons) to work with the image. In addition to using these toolbar buttons, you can also use menu commands to accomplish tasks. Check your scanner program manual for specific instructions on how to open and work with scanned images.

You can also open the image in an image-editing program, such as Photoshop Elements (see Figure 4-3), and use this program's tools to edit the image. Chapter 5 covers how to open and modify an image, including scanned images.

Figure 4-3 A scanned image opened in Photoshop Elements. The scanned image is now ready for you to enhance and manipulate.

Troubleshooting Hardware Problems

If you're having problems with your camera or scanner, you can use Windows Troubleshooter to pinpoint the exact problem and view possible solutions. For instance, perhaps you can't access your camera's images, or maybe you can't scan because the scanner is not connected correctly.

To use Windows Troubleshooter to get solutions to common problems, follow these steps:

1 Click the **start** button, and then right-click **My Computer** in the start menu. A shortcut menu appears.

 Be sure to right-click **My Computer**. If you left-click it, you'll see the contents of the My Computer folder instead of a shortcut menu.

2 Click **Properties** to display the System Properties dialog box.

3 Click the **Hardware** tab to view the list of options.

4 Click the **Device Manager** button. The Device Manager window opens.

5 If you are having problems with a digital camera, click the **plus sign** next to Disk Drives. If you are having problems with a scanner, click the **plus sign** next to the Imaging Devices entry. The Imaging Devices or Disk Drives list will expand; you should see your camera or scanner listed.

 If your device is not listed, it has not yet been installed. If this is the case, reinstall the scanner or camera.

6 Right-click your device and click **Properties** in the shortcut menu that appears. The Properties dialog box opens with its General tab displayed. This tab lists information about your camera or scanner.

7 Click **Troubleshoot** to start the Troubleshooting Wizard. The Windows Help and Support Center window will open.

8 Click **I am having a problem with my scanner/camera**, and then select **Next**.

9. Read the help information that appears and select options to focus on the problems your scanner or camera may be experiencing. For example, if you are troubleshooting a problem with your scanner, Windows first asks what type of scanner you are using (that is, how it is attached). Click **Parallel Port or USB**, and then click **Next**.

10. Windows then asks you to double-check that the device is turned on and connected; do so and click **Next**.

11. Follow each step, clicking **Next** to advance to the next screen, until you pinpoint and solve the problem using the suggestions in the Troubleshooter.

12. Click the **Close** button to close the Help and Support Center window.

Managing Photos in Windows XP

4

Chances are, you use a filing cabinet at work or home to organize and protect important papers and other items. Most likely, this filing cabinet features two or more drawers, and each drawer contains folders. Each folder is labeled and contains any number of related documents. For example, you might have a folder labeled "Tax Return" that contains all your important receipts, bank statements, and a copy of the tax return you sent to the IRS.

Your computer's hard disk acts somewhat like a filing cabinet in that it enables you to "file" your important documents—including digital images—in folders. Some of these folders, such as My Pictures, are created automatically by your computer's operating system; others you create yourself. You can even create subfolders and place them in other folders. When you use an organized folder structure, locating your digital images is easy.

In this section, you'll learn how to use Windows XP to organize your digital images. You'll learn how to manage your files by using folders to group related images, by giving your images descriptive names, and by deleting unwanted images.

 Windows XP comes with a built-in thumbnail viewer so you can see small versions of your images in the My Computer interface. To use this setting, click **start** and choose **My Computer**. In the My Computer window, select **Thumbnails** from the View menu.

Creating Folders

As mentioned previously, many versions of Windows (including Windows XP) include a special folder called My Pictures. One way to organize your photos is to store them all in this folder, much like some people store their photos in a shoebox. Doing this is certainly convenient, but just as digging through a shoebox to find a particular print can be time-consuming, so is sifting through image files in a folder to find the one you want.

 If Get pictures from camera or scanner is not available, to retrieve images click **start**, then **My Computer**. Right-click the **Removable Drive** icon and choose **AutoPlay**. Then select **Copy pictures to a folder on my computer using Microsoft Scanner and Camera Wizard**.

To remedy this problem, you can create subfolders within the My Pictures folder (or any other folder). For example, you might have one folder named "Trip to Paris," and in it you could store all the pictures from your recent visit to the City of Lights. You might have another folder named "Rover," containing all your digital photos of your dog. Or if you're putting together a scrapbook for a family reunion, you could store all the photos for that event in a "Reunion" folder. If your photos are well organized, you can easily find images you want to use without conducting exhaustive searches through the recesses of your hard drive.

To create a folder within My Pictures (or any other folder you choose) in Windows XP, follow these steps:

❶ To open the My Pictures folder, click **start** and select **My Pictures**.

❷ Click **Make a new folder** in the task pane. Alternatively, you can click **File**, **New**, and then **Folder**. A new folder will be created within the My Pictures folder.

❸ Type a descriptive name to replace the default name of "New Folder," and then press **ENTER**. (New Folder is already selected, so you can start typing the new name immediately.)

After you create a new folder, you can use it to store images or any other type of document or program. In fact, it's a good idea to create several folders in this manner and give each one a descriptive name; that way, you can organize your images into the various folders to keep track of them.

Finding, Moving, and Copying Files

If you've already transferred photos from your digital camera to your hard drive, the images were most likely placed in a folder created by your digital camera software. The same goes for digital images you created using a scanner—the scanner software probably placed your scanned images in its own proprietary folder.

Fortunately, you can move those files easily from their default locations to almost any other folder on your hard drive, including the one you created in the preceding section. Rather than move files, you might decide to copy them from one folder to another so you have extra copies in case you need them.

Before you can organize your image files, you must first find them. If you're not certain where your digital camera or scanner places image files by default, you can use Windows XP's Search Companion feature to quickly locate them. To use Search Companion, follow these steps:

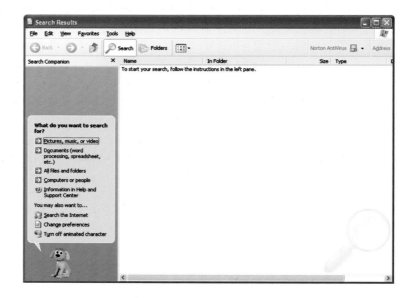

1 Click **start** and choose **Search**. The Search Results window opens.

2 Click **Pictures, music, or video** under What do you want to search for?

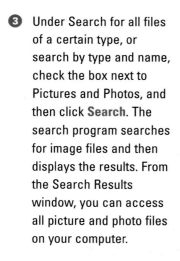

3 Under Search for all files of a certain type, or search by type and name, check the box next to Pictures and Photos, and then click **Search**. The search program searches for image files and then displays the results. From the Search Results window, you can access all picture and photo files on your computer.

When you've found your image files, you can use Windows XP to move one or more of them to another folder on your hard disk.

① Locate and open the folder that contains the file or files you want to move.

② Click any file you want to move. To select several files, hold down the **CTRL** key on your keyboard while clicking each file you want to move. If the files you want to move are adjacent in the file list, you can select them all by holding down the **SHIFT** key on your keyboard and clicking the first and last file you want to move.

 If you want to move an entire folder and its contents to another location, simply click the folder you want to move and then move it as you would any file. Use the method outlined previously to select multiple folders—just click folders instead of files.

③ Click **Move this file** (or **Move this folder** if you selected a folder) in the File and Folder Tasks portion of the task pane on the left side of the window. (If you selected multiple files, click **Move selected items**.) The Move Items dialog box opens.

④ Click the folder into which you want to move the file(s) or folder(s). To locate the folder, click the **plus sign** next to the drive in which the folder resides. If the folder is a subfolder, click the **plus sign** next to its parent folder to display it.

 If you haven't created a folder yet for your image files, you can do so by clicking on the drive or folder in which you want the new folder to reside. Then click on **Make New Folder**, type a descriptive name for the folder, and press **ENTER**.

⑤ Click **Move**. The file(s) or folder(s) will be moved to the folder you selected in Step 4.

 If you prefer, you can click **Edit** and choose **Cut** to delete files or folders from their current location and copy them to the Windows XP Clipboard. Then, in the folder in which you want to place the images or folders, click **Edit** and choose **Paste**.

Copying files in Windows XP is similar to moving them. Here's how it's done:

1 Locate and open the folder that contains the file(s) or folder(s) you want to copy.

2 Click the file(s) or folder(s) you want to copy. (Refer to Step 2 of the preceding exercise for information about selecting multiple files or folders.)

3 In the task pane, click **Copy this file** (to copy a single file) or **Copy the selected items** (to copy multiple files). The Copy Items dialog box will open.

4 In the Copy Items dialog box, click the folder into which you want to copy the files. (For help locating the folder, refer to Step 4 of the preceding exercise.)

As with the Move Items dialog box, you can use the Copy Items dialog box to create new folders. Click on the drive or folder in which you want the new folder to reside, and then click **Make New Folder**, type a descriptive name for the folder, and press **ENTER**.

❺ Click **Copy**. The files will be copied to the folder you selected in Step 4.

 As with moving files, you can use the Edit menu commands to copy files and folders from one folder to another. Simply click **Copy** instead of Cut and continue as in the preceding exercise.

Renaming Files

You've managed to move your digital images from their original location to the folders you've created. But how can you tell which one is which? Thanks to your digital camera or scanner's rather bland default naming scheme, the names of your image files just aren't very descriptive—at best, they contain the date the photo was taken and little else. If you transfer or scan two images on the same date, the program simply appends a number to the file name to distinguish the files, such as "Sunday May 18 (2)." Some devices provide file names as nondescript as "Image001."

If you don't change the names of these files, locating one you need later can be tiresome. That's why it's a good idea to develop a naming scheme for your image files. One possibility is to name your image files after the subjects of the photographs, plus the date or event where the photo was taken. For example, rather than leave an image file with the default name "Sunday May 18 (2)," you might name it "Gramps Family Reunion" so you know the picture is of Gramps at your family reunion. If you took several pictures of Gramps, you could number each one within your naming scheme, as in "GrampsFamilyReunion1," "GrampsFamilyReunion2," and so on. Alternatively, you might decide to base your naming scheme on the folder that contains the images you want to rename. Using the family reunion example, you might create a folder named "Family Reunion" and then name the photos in that folder "FamilyReunion1," "FamilyReunion2," and so on.

 Renaming your image files does more than help you find the ones you like; it also helps to prevent you from accidentally deleting files you want to keep.

To rename files in Windows XP, follow these steps:

❶ Open the folder that contains files you want to rename.
❷ Click an image you want to rename. (You can rename only one file at a time.)

❸ In the task pane, click **Rename this file**. (Alternatively, you can right-click the file and click **Rename** in the shortcut menu that appears.)

❹ The filename will selected; type a new name and press **ENTER** to rename the file.

Of course, finding a naming scheme that is specific enough for you to identify the file you want on the first try is a bit difficult. Fortunately, Windows XP enables you to view a small version of each image in a folder (called a thumbnail) alongside its file name. That way, if you have several photos of Gramps at the family reunion, you can scan these thumbnail images to locate the one you want. To configure Windows XP to display thumbnails of each image file in a folder, you simply change to Thumbnail view; to do so, click **View** and select **Thumbnail**.

Deleting Files

Digital image files are very large and can quickly fill up your hard drive. For this reason, it's a good idea to delete any image files you no longer need. Alternatively, you can copy your image files to a CD or some other media, as discussed in the "Archiving Your Digital Images" section, and delete them from your hard drive to make room for new files.

You can delete one or more files at a time in Windows XP, and you can also delete folders. Here's how:

 When you delete a folder, you also delete all its contents.

❶ Locate and open the folder that contains the file or files you want to delete.

② Click the file(s) or folder(s) you want to delete. To select several files or folders, hold down the **CTRL** key on your keyboard while you click each file or folder you want to delete. If the files or folders are adjacent in the list, you can select them all by holding down the **SHIFT** key on your keyboard and clicking the first and last file or folder you want to delete.

③ In the task pane, click **Delete this file** (for a single file), **Delete selected items** (for multiple files or folders), or **Delete this folder** (for a folder). Alternatively, right-click a selected file or folder and click **Delete** in the shortcut menu that appears.

④ Windows XP asks you to confirm that you want to delete the selected files or folders. Click **Yes**.

When you delete files or folders in Windows XP, they're not removed from your hard drive right away; instead, they are moved to the Recycle Bin, a temporary storage location for recently deleted files. You use the Recycle Bin like the wastebasket beside your desk. If you throw away a paper document and decide later that you should keep it, you can always pull it out of the wastebasket—until you empty your trash. Likewise, if you delete a file, you can recover it until you tell Windows to empty the Recycle Bin (or until Windows runs out of room in the Recycle Bin and permanently deletes the files in it to free up space).

 If you've deleted any files in error, you can retrieve them from the Recycle Bin. Simply double-click the **Recycle Bin** on your desktop to open the Recycle Bin window. Then select the file you want to restore and click **Restore this item**. If you have selected multiple items, click **Restore the selected items**. With no selection, click **Restore all items** to retrieve all files from the Recycle Bin.

Because your goal in deleting your digital image files is to free up space on your hard drive, you'll need to empty the Recycle Bin to seal the deal. To do so, simply double-click the **Recycle Bin** on your desktop to open the Recycle Bin window. Then click **Empty the recycle bin**. When prompted, click **Yes** to confirm that you want to permanently delete all items in the Recycle Bin.

 Once you've emptied the Recycle Bin, you cannot retrieve any files you've deleted.

Using Image-Management Software

In addition to using Windows XP to manage and organize your images, you can also use image-management software specifically designed to help you organize your photo collection. Using one of these programs, such as Adobe Photoshop Album (see Figure 4-4), you can easily find, consolidate, and organize images on your computer and images imported from a scanner or digital camera. You can also create albums, slideshows, and even Web pages with ease.

Figure 4-4 Adobe Photoshop Album is one image-management program.

Before you can take advantage of an image-management program, you need to instruct the software to acquire, or import, the images. Importing images that are already on your computer into Photoshop Album is easy. Just follow these steps:

1 From the **File** menu, choose **Get Photos**, and then select **By Searching**.

2 The Get Photos By Searching for Folders dialog box will appear. Click on the **Look in** drop-down menu and choose the location you want to search for image files. Choose **All Hard Disks** to search your entire computer. Alternatively, you could look in a specific drive or folder.

3 Click **Search**. All folders in the location you selected that contain image files will appear in the Search Results list. Click a folder to preview its contents.

4 Click **Import Folders** to open the image files in the main Photoshop Album window for further management or to perform other operations.

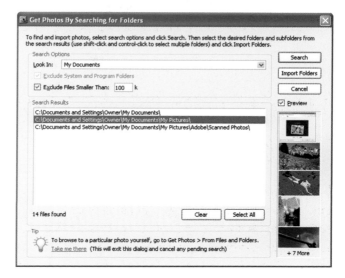

To import images directly from a digital camera, card reader, or scanner, click the **File** menu, choose **Get Photos**, and then select **From camera or card reader or from scanner**. Importing images directly from a scanner was covered earlier, in the "Scanning an Image" section.

Organizing Images with Photoshop Album

After you have consolidated your photos, it's time to assign them to categories. By adding some custom information to your photographs, Photoshop Album can make organizing them and finding them later a snap. Computers are best at finding files by looking at the size or file name, but you are more capable of distinguishing pictures you took on Barbados versus those you took on the Virgin Islands. For this reason, Photoshop Album lets you create your own categories and assign each picture in your collection to one of these categories. A category you assign to a file is called a tag, and this assignment will define some characteristic of the file. You can use categories such as People, Places, Family, or any criteria you want to use that will help you find the picture later. After you have established the criteria and tagged your photos accordingly, you'll find it easy to track down any of your photos. In this section, you'll learn how to create tags, assign your photos, and then search for photos using the criteria you assigned.

Creating a Tag

A number of tags are defined for you already, including People, Places, Family, and so on. However, you probably need additional tags to encompass the variety of photos in your collection. To create your own tag, follow these steps:

1 From the Tag menu, choose **New Tag**.

2 In the Tag Editor dialog box, choose a category, and then enter a tag name (and a note if desired), as shown in Figure 4-5.

 To create your own sub-category, choose **Sub-Category** from the **Tags** menu.

3 Click **OK**. Now you can assign photos to the tag you created, which will be covered next.

Figure 4-5 In Photoshop Album, create tags to categorize your photos.

Assigning Tags to Photos

To assign a tag to a photo, simply right-click the thumbnail in the main window, and then choose **Attach Tag**, followed by the appropriate submenu item, and then the tag. For example, as shown in Figure 4-6, to assign an image to the Caribbean tag, right-click the image and choose **Attach Tag, Places, Caribbean**.

Figure 4-6 Right-click to assign a tag to an image.

Using Tags to Find Photos

After you have tagged photos under a category, it's easy to find them in the future. From the View menu, choose **Tags**. (Alternatively, you can press Ctrl+T.) This opens the Tags pane on the left side of your screen (refer to Figure 4-6). Simply click the down arrow next to a sub-category to view the tags, and then click the box to the left of the tag to display all the images assigned to that tag in the main window on the right side of the screen.

 In addition to using tags, there are many other ways to hunt down image files using Photoshop Album. In fact, the entire Find menu is designated for all of the available search functions. However, personally assigning your own tags is the best way to keep track of your photos.

Other Benefits of Image-Management Software

In addition to the convenience of managing all of your images in one place, there are a variety of other advantages to using image-management software. For example, you can generate slideshows and albums with a single command. Photoshop Album then runs a wizard that asks you how to display your pictures, and with what style of background. The results can be sent to a friend over e-mail, archived on a CD, or posted to a Web site. You'll learn more about creating digital albums and slideshows, as well as other features offered by image-management software, in Chapter 6, "Doing More with Your Photos."

Archiving Your Digital Images

Just as you might keep negatives of your pictures as an archive in case something happens to your prints, you can also archive your original digital image files. One major reason to do so is that image files are large and consume significant space. When you archive your digital image files, you free up space on your hard drive, making room for other files. Another major reason to archive files is for protection: You can archive your favorite image files as backups in case the original files become damaged.

One way to archive your digital image files is to keep them on your hard drive in a compressed format; that way, they consume considerably less space. Alternatively, if your computer has a drive that lets you record CDs, you can copy your image files to a CD and archive them that way. The next two sections discuss these options.

Archiving Images on Your Hard Drive

No matter how large your hard drive is, it will fill up if you add large numbers of image files to it. One solution is to add another drive to gain more disk space. Another solution is to store your images in a compressed (or zipped) folder. That way, the images remain on your hard drive, but in a different, more compact format.

 In addition to the compression utility included with Windows XP, you can download programs from the Internet to compress files. These include shareware programs, for which you pay a small fee, and freeware programs, which are free.

To use Windows XP to store images in a compressed folder, follow these steps:

❶ Locate and open the folder that contains any images you want to compress.

❷ Click the image(s) or folder(s) you want to compress. (To select multiple images or folders, hold down the **CTRL** key while you click each item you want to compress. To select a contiguous list of files or folders to compress, hold down the **SHIFT** key while you click the first and last file or folder in the range.)

❸ Right-click any of the selected files, choose **Send to** from the shortcut menu that appears, and click **Compressed (zipped) Folder**. Windows XP's built-in compression utility will compress and store the images in a compressed folder within the current folder. A progress window will indicate the progress of the compression operation.

④ The compressed folder's default name usually consists of the name of one of the compressed images. To give the compressed folder a more descriptive name, right-click it and choose **Rename** from the shortcut menu that appears. The folder's name will be selected.

⑤ Type a new name for the folder and press **ENTER**.

When you send images to a compressed folder, they are copied, not moved. That means the original image files remain on the disk. To free up disk space, delete the original versions of the images you compressed. (To select multiple images, hold down the **CTRL** key while you click on each file you want to delete. Or, hold down the **SHIFT** key to select a range of contiguous files.)

 As mentioned earlier in this chapter, files or folders that are deleted are not removed from your system; they are moved to the Recycle Bin, where they continue to consume disk space. To permanently remove the files from your system, you must empty the Recycle Bin. For help performing this task, refer to the "Deleting Files" section earlier in this chapter.

4

Although you can't open images when they're compressed, you can decompress or extract them when you want to work with them. To do so, follow these steps:

① Locate and open the folder that contains the compressed folder with the images you want to extract.

② Double-click the compressed folder. Its contents will be displayed in a window, but the files aren't yet extracted.

③ Select the file(s) you want to extract.

④ Right-click any one of the selected files and click **Copy** in the shortcut menu that appears.

⑤ Open the folder or drive to which you want to copy the files.

6 Right-click in a blank area of the folder window and click **Paste** in the shortcut menu that appears. The files will be extracted and copied to the open folder.

 Don't close the window with the compressed files before pasting them. If you close a compressed folder, copied contents are erased from the clipboard.

If you want to extract all the files in the folder, click **Extract All Files** in the compressed folder window's task pane. This will start the Compressed (Zipped) Folders Extraction Wizard. Read the Welcome screen and click **Next**. When prompted, select the folder in which you want to place the extracted images, and then click **Finish**. The images will be extracted and copied to the folder you selected.

Saving Images on a CD

CD-ROM drives have been standard equipment on most computers for nearly a decade, making it easy to install programs, view data, and so on. However, CD-ROM drives have one major limitation. Although they can read data from discs, they can't write data to discs—you can't use a CD-ROM drive to save data on a CD.

In recent years, technology has given rise to a new generation of recordable CD drives that not only read data from discs, but also record data to discs. In other words, if you insert a blank CD into a recordable CD drive, you can copy information from your computer to the disc. With a recordable CD drive, you can back up data files (including image files) to CDs, allowing you to free up even more hard-drive space than you can free when you compress image files.

 The advantage of using CDs instead of other storage media, such as floppy disks, to store your digital images is that CDs can store anywhere from 650 to 700 MB of data—the equivalent of nearly 500 floppy disks! This provides ample storage for your digital images.

There are two different types of recordable CD drives:

✦ **CD-R drives.** A CD-R drive (R for read) can read data from CD-ROM discs and write to CD-R discs. A CD-R disc is a CD on which you can save or write data one time only. Once it has been written to, a CD-R becomes a CD-ROM.

✦ **CD-RW drives.** A CD-RW drive (RW for read-write) has the same capabilities as a CD-R drive, but you can use it to record data to the same CD multiple times. You can even erase a CD and reuse it. To take advantage of these additional capabilities, you must use a special type of CD called a CD-RW.

You can also record image files to DVDs (Digital Video Discs) if you have a recordable DVD drive installed on your computer. DVDs can hold up to 6 GB of data, the equivalent of nearly nine CDs.

You can use Windows XP to copy your images to a CD just as you would use it to copy to any other type of drive. In addition to enabling you to archive images you no longer need, copying images to a CD is a good way to create backups of your important image files—the ones you really don't want damaged or lost. If you want, you can archive copies of these files on CD, leaving the original versions intact on your computer. Here's how:

 Some recordable CD drives come bundled with their own software for writing data to a CD (a process also known as burning a CD). Consult the user guide that came with your computer to find out whether your drive requires you to use its accompanying software instead of Windows XP to burn files to CD.

① Insert a blank CD into the recordable CD drive. The CD Drive dialog box will appear. Click **Cancel**.

② Click **start** and select **My Computer**. The My Computer window will open.

③ Locate and open the drive and folder that contain the image files you want to copy to CD.

④ Select the file or files you want to copy.

⑤ The next step depends on the folder in which your image files are stored. If your pictures are stored in the My Pictures folder, click **Copy to CD** in the task pane. If your pictures are stored in another folder, click **Copy this file** (for a single file), **Copy this folder** (for a folder), or **Copy the selected items** (for multiple files). The Copy Items dialog box will open.

⑥ Click the CD-R or CD-RW drive, and then click **Copy**. The files will be copied to the CD-R or CD-RW drive.

 You can purchase blank CDs at computer stores, office supply stores, warehouse stores, and other places. Remember: CD-R drives can write only to CD-R discs, but CD-RW drives can write to both CD-R and CD-RW discs. DVD recorder drives require media designed for the type of DVD burner. For example, DVD-RAM drives can burn DVD-RAM discs, but not other types of recordable DVDs. DVD-RAM drives are also capable of recording CD-R and CD-RW discs and can read information from discs of any of these formats.

Because you have copied the files rather than moved them, they are still taking up space on your hard drive. To free up this space, empty the Recycle Bin. (For help deleting image files and emptying the Recycle Bin, refer to the "Deleting Files" section earlier in this chapter.) Alternatively, you can leave the originals intact and save the files on CD or DVD as a backup in the event that the original files are damaged or deleted.

Other Tips for Managing Your Images

Now that you have learned the fundamentals of managing your digital images, here are some other tips you might find helpful:

✦ Use high-capacity removable media. Memory cards capable of storing 512 MB and more have recently become more affordable than ever. Also, high-resolution images of 3, 4, and 5 megapixels take up a lot of space on a media card, so having a small amount of memory can be a real inconvenience. Having more memory allows you to store more images on your camera before you move them to your computer, and it gives you the freedom to shoot images at a higher resolution without filling the card too quickly.

✦ If you plan to take many pictures before you move them to your computer (which might be the case while you're on vacation, for example), consider carrying two or more memory cards with you.

✦ If you find yourself needing several memory cards to store your images in the field, you might consider purchasing a battery-powered portable hard drive to store your images. These devices can offer from 3 to 30 GB of storage space and are usually compatible with some type of removable media, like CompactFlash or SmartMedia. These devices can also usually transfer data directly to a computer through a USB or FireWire connection.

✦ If you have a number of portable devices that use removable media, you might consider using a universal card reader. These devices connect to your computer, usually with a USB or FireWire cable, and can transfer data from a variety of media cards to your computer. One such memory card reader, Dazzle, shown in Figure 4-7, is capable of reading CompactFlash, IBM Microdrive, SmartMedia, Sony Memory Stick, MultiMediaCard, and SD cards.

Figure 4-7 The Dazzle universal memory card reader is capable of transferring images to your computer from six different types of removable media.

Editing and Manipulating Your Images

Everyone has that one photograph that simply got away. Sometimes the photograph eludes you because you didn't have your camera with you. Other times you manage to snap the scene, only to discover that your thumb was covering the edge of the lens.

Image-editing software can't help you if you missed a shot because you forgot your camera. It can, however, rectify photographic mistakes like the thumb. Using image-editing software, you can crop out the offending digit, as well as correct images that are too dark or too bright, fix red-eye, rotate images, and more. In addition, you can use image-editing software to apply a wide variety of special effects to your images. In this chapter. you'll gain an overview of what you can accomplish using your photo-editing program, and you'll learn some specific skills that will help you perfect your images.

Understanding Image Editing Basics

In Chapter 2, you were introduced to some image-editing programs. Many digital cameras or camera bundles include an image-editing program that will probably work perfectly for your needs. But if your camera doesn't include an editing program, or if you think you'd prefer to use a different program, you can also buy one. Although each image-editing program on the market works a little bit differently, most offer the same basic set of features. For example, nearly every program enables you to open, edit, organize, share, and print your pictures. However, image-editing programs often differ in precisely how you accomplish each of these actions.

In this section, you'll learn some common characteristics of image-editing software and preview some of the tools you can expect to find in such a software package.

 This chapter provides detailed steps for tasks using Photoshop Elements and Picture It!. If you use a different program, check its user guide for specific instructions. Typically, the steps are very similar.

Before you can use your image-editing program, you must first install it. The specific steps for this process differ from program to program. Usually you can simply insert the CD into your CD drive and follow the directions. If you have problems with installation, consult the program's manual for additional instructions. After you install your image-editing program, you start it just as you would any other program.

When you start your image-editing program, it will probably display a Welcome screen with icons and/or links (underlined menu commands) for common tasks. This Welcome screen can help you familiarize yourself with your image-editing program. For example, Photoshop Elements displays a Welcome screen with options for opening a file on your computer, connecting to a camera or scanner, and going through a tutorial (see Figure 5-1).

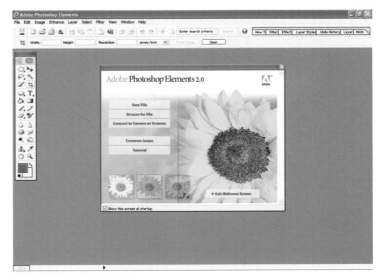

Figure 5-1 Open a file, import an image from your camera or scanner, or go through a tutorial from the Photoshop Elements Welcome screen.

 In Photoshop Elements, as in some other image-editing programs, the Welcome screen appears each time you start the program unless you remove the checkmark from the Show This Screen at Startup box in the lower-left corner.

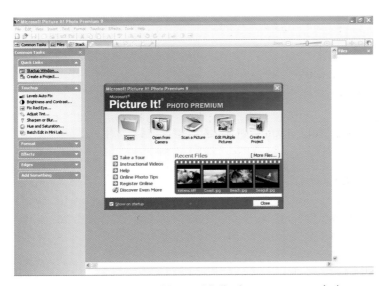

Figure 5-2 When launched, Picture It! displays a startup window that contains various options for opening files and viewing reference materials.

Likewise, Picture It! displays a Welcome screen upon startup, listing your main choices: Open, Open from Camera, Scan a Picture, Edit Multiple Pictures, or Create a Project (see Figure 5-2). From this screen, you can also take a tour of the program and access help and reference materials. Also, recently opened images appear in this window for easy access.

Opening and Saving Your Images

Now that you're familiar with your image editor's program window and tools, it's time to get down to the business of using the program to work with your images. First, however, you must learn how to open images on your computer.

Before you can open an image on your computer, you must download it from your digital camera, scan it using your scanner, or obtain it in some other way—perhaps by downloading it from the Internet or copying it from a photo CD. In many cases, you can use your image-editing program to complete this task. When the image is stored on your computer, you can use your image-editing program to open it.

In this section, you'll learn how to open images stored on your computer and save the changes you make to an image.

Opening an Image for Editing

Chapter 1 discussed the many different sources for digital images, including digital cameras, scanners, the Internet, and your computer. Most image-editing programs enable you to obtain pictures from the following sources:

+ **Your computer.** In most cases, you transfer images from your digital camera or other device, such as a scanner, directly to your computer. You probably store images found on the Internet on your computer as well.
You can use your image-editing program to open image files directly from your computer. When you choose this method, you select the drive and folder where your images are stored, including your CD-ROM drive, and then open the images.

+ **Your digital camera.** Many image-editing programs enable you to download and open pictures directly from your camera. For help transferring pictures from your camera to your computer, review Chapter 3.

+ **Your scanner.** In most cases, you can start a scan from your image-editing program and scan the image directly into the image-editing program window. The option for doing this might be called Scanner or TWAIN.

TWAIN is the official technical standard for scanning images. Almost all scanners come with a TWAIN driver (software that allows the device to communicate with the computer). This makes such scanners compatible with any other device that supports the TWAIN standard.

✦ **The Internet.** You can use your image-editing program to access online photo and image sources and download image files to your computer.

Let's take a look at the most common method of opening pictures—from the computer. The following sections cover opening images using Photoshop Elements and Picture It!.

 Often you may want to open and work with several pictures at once or in order. Most programs enable you to open a set of pictures and select the image you want to work with first. The image you've selected appears in the image-editing program's work area, and the remaining images are displayed in a library or Files palette. In the following sections, you'll learn how to open and manage multiple images.

Opening an Image in Photoshop Elements

To use Photoshop Elements to open an image stored on your computer, follow these steps:

❶ On the Welcome screen, click **Browse for File**. The File Browser dialog box will appear; it will display the contents of the My Pictures folder automatically.

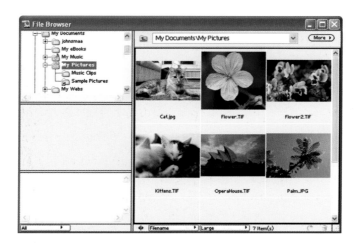

❷ Navigate to the file using the folder list in the upper-right corner of the dialog box. Click the + (plus sign) to the left of a folder to expand it; click the – (minus sign) to the left of a folder to collapse it. Click a folder to display its contents in the preview pane on the right side of the dialog box.

By default, most image-editing programs only list image files when you browse for files to open. Photoshop Elements automatically filters out word processing documents, digital music files, and other file types, which makes finding images easier.

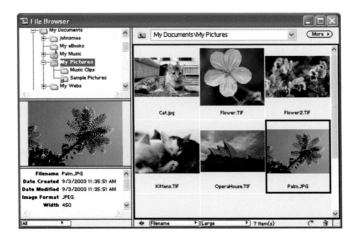

❸ Click the image file you want to open. The image and additional file information will appear in the preview area beneath the folder list. To select multiple files, hold down the **CTRL** key and click each file you want to open. If you select multiple images, no preview will be displayed in the left preview pane.

❹ Double-click a selected file to open all selected files; or, right-click a file and choose **Open**. If you selected a single image file, it will open in the work area. If you selected multiple files, they will all open in the work area.

Opening an Image in Picture It!

Follow these steps to open an image using Picture It!:

❶ On the Welcome screen, click **Open**. The File Browser dialog box will appear.

Picture It! also lists recently opened files on the Welcome screen; you can reopen these files by clicking on them.

❷ Using the list on the left side of the dialog box, locate the folder that contains your image files. Click the + (plus sign) to the left of a folder to expand it; click the − (minus sign) to the left of a folder to collapse it. Click a folder to display its contents in the preview pane on the right side of the dialog box.

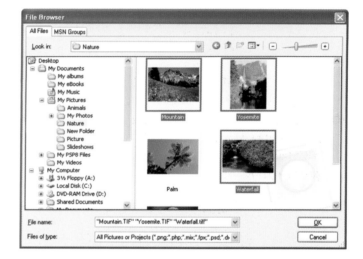

❸ On the right side of the File Browser dialog box, click the image file you want to open. To select multiple files, hold down the **CTRL** key and click each file you want to open.

5

❹ Click **OK**. If you selected a single image file, it will open in the work area. If you selected multiple files, click the **Files** button in the upper-left corner of the screen to show the Files palette, which displays all opened files to the right of the main project area.

Saving an Image

In most cases, before you begin to make changes to an open image, you should create a working copy of it. That way, any changes you make to the image will occur on the working copy, while the original remains intact. You can then save the copy as a new file with a different name than the original. If your edits are disappointing, this ensures that you can always return to the original and start over.

When you save an image file, observe the following guidelines:

✦ **Select the correct command from the File menu.** Choose **Save As** the first time you save the file, and give it a new name or store it in a new location, thereby preserving the original. After you've saved the file using the Save As command, click **Save** periodically as you continue to edit the image.

Don't wait until you've put the final touches on your image to save it, and be sure to keep saving as you work. Otherwise, if some disaster befell your computer (for instance, if it lost power), all your work would be lost.

✦ **Rename downloaded images.** When you download pictures from a digital camera, the file names are usually not very descriptive. For example, images might be named according to the date they were taken, or the camera might use a numbering scheme to identify the order in which they were taken. To help you remember which image is which, it's a good idea to save each image file using a descriptive file name.

Even if you don't open pictures for editing and then save them, you should still rename your files if their names are not descriptive. This will help you keep your image files organized. As you learned in Chapter 4, you can rename files in a Windows folder by right-clicking the file, selecting **Rename** from the menu that appears, and typing a new name.

✦ **Select a file format.** If your image-editing program saves image files using a default proprietary file format, you might decide to change a file's format to share it with people who use different image-editing programs. The JPEG format is used frequently for images placed on the Web because JPEG images are compressed and therefore require less space. The TIF and PCX formats are used commonly for printed illustrations. For more information about file formats, refer to Chapter 4. To change the file type, click the **Save as Type** drop-down menu, and then select the format you want.

Both Photoshop Elements and Picture It! include many options for saving, including saving a project or an album. You'll learn about some of these additional features in Chapter 6, "Doing More with Your Photos."

Saving an Image in Photoshop Elements

To save an image that is open in the Photoshop Elements work area, follow these steps:

1 Click **File**, and then click **Save As**. The Save As dialog box will open.

2 Navigate to the drive and folder where you want to store your image.

3 Locate and open the folder in which you want to save your image.

 If you want to create a new folder for your images, click the drive or folder in which you want to place the new folder, and then click **Create New Folder**. The new folder will appear. Type a name for the folder and press **ENTER**. Double-click the new folder to open it.

4 Type a name for the file in the File name text box. Make sure this name describes the contents of the image file.

5 Click **Save**.

Saving an Image in Picture It!

To save an image that is open in the Picture It! work area, follow these steps:

1 Click **File**, and then click **Save as** to open the Save As dialog box.

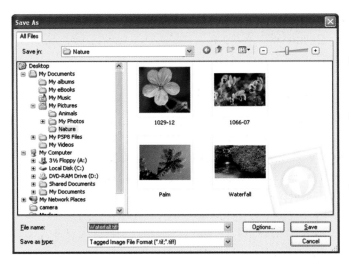

② Locate and open the folder in which you want to save your image.

③ Type a file name in the File name text box. Make sure this name describes the contents of the image file.

④ Click **Save**.

Enhancing Pictures

Now that you understand the basics of your image-editing program, it's time to get into the meat of the program—using it to enhance your images.

One of the most common reasons to edit an image is to correct problems in it. For example, you might discover that the image is too light or too dark, that it lacks contrast, or that the eyes of your photograph's subject may appear to be red, a common problem with flash photography. You might want to eliminate unwanted elements of the picture and keep only part of it. In this section, you'll learn how to correct these common problems.

 Most image-editing programs offer many more tools for fixing problem pictures than the ones covered here. For information about some other types of enhancements you might be able to apply using your image editor, see Chapter 6.

Adjusting Color

Many factors affect the color in your image, including brightness, contrast, and tint. If your picture is too dark, you can use your image-editing program to brighten it. Or perhaps the details in your image are not sharp—in that case, you can adjust the image's contrast. Finally, if you want to add a special effect, you can adjust an image's tint. In this section, you'll learn how to adjust basic color settings using Photoshop Elements and Picture It!

Every picture is different, so there are no set rules for determining what color settings will work best for you. To get the color in your image just right, you'll need to experiment a bit with the various settings. Don't be afraid; you can always undo your edits if you don't like the results. You'll learn how to undo changes to an image file later in this chapter, in the "Undoing Editing Changes" section.

Enhancing Color in Photoshop Elements

Photoshop Elements can adjust the color, brightness, and contrast of your image automatically, or you can use the program to adjust the color manually. It's always best to try the automatic features first to let the software do the work for you. Then, if you don't like the results, you can adjust the settings manually. To instruct Photoshop Elements to handle color and contrast settings automatically, follow these steps:

1 Make sure the image you want to change is open in the Photoshop Elements work area.

2 From the Enhance menu, choose **Auto Levels, Auto Contrast,** or **Auto Color Correction**. When you choose one of these options, Photoshop Elements takes the necessary steps to enhance the image's color settings. Figure 5-3 demonstrates an image before and after these automatic enhancements.

3 To reject these changes, choose **Undo** from the Edit menu (or press **CTRL+Z**).

Figure 5-3 Using Auto Levels, Auto Contrast, and Auto Color Correction you can easily improve the appearance of your photographs.

To adjust the color settings manually, you can use Photoshop Element's Quick Fix utility. Using this method, you can apply to your image several effects related to color, brightness, and contrast before you confirm your changes.

 If an area is selected, Quick Fix applies changes to the selected area only. You'll learn about selection in the "Cropping an Image" section later in this chapter.

To use Photoshop Elements' Quick Fix feature to adjust color settings, follow these steps:

1 Make sure the image you want to change is open in the work area.

2 From the Enhance menu, choose **Quick Fix**. The Quick Fix dialog box will appear.

3 In the Select Adjustment Category section, choose **Brightness** or **Color Correction**.

 In addition to color and brightness, you can adjust focus and rotation settings from the Quick Fix dialog box. You will learn more about these features later in this chapter, in the "Rotating an Image" and "Adding Other Special Effects" sections.

4 In the Select Adjustment section, choose the desired effect. For example, choose **Brightness/Contrast** to compensate for exposure problems.

5 In the third column, your options will depend on the adjustment you selected. Click the **Apply** button. Alternatively, you can click and drag a slider to preview the adjustment in the preview pane at the top of the Quick Fix dialog box. Figure 5-4 demonstrates how you can improve brightness by using Quick Fix.

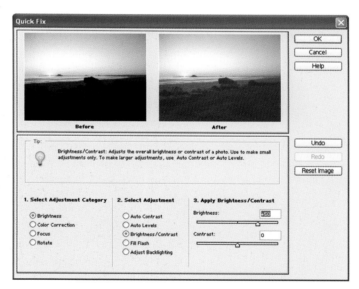

Figure 5-4 Adjust the color and brightness using Photoshop Elements' Quick Fix feature.

6 Click the **Undo** button to undo the previous change. Click the **Reset** button to revert to the original image. Click **OK** to accept the changes and return to the main window.

Adjusting Color in Picture It!

Like Photoshop Elements, Picture It! affords you several options when it comes to adjusting the color in your image—and using them is just as easy. For example, to adjust image brightness and contrast automatically, follow these simple steps:

① Make sure the image you want to change is open in the Picture It! work area.

② In the Common Tasks pane on the left side of the screen, open the **Touchup pane** (if it's not already open).

③ Choose **Brightness and Contrast**. The Brightness and Contrast task pane will open.

④ Click **Levels auto fix** and **Contrast auto fix**. Picture It! will update the image, correcting brightness and contrast problems automatically. Figure 5-5 demonstrates these results.

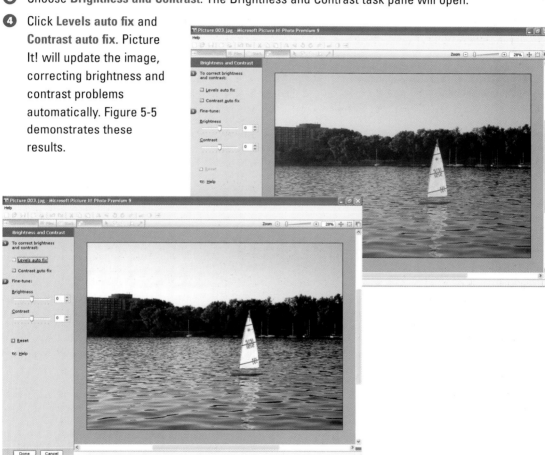

Figure 5-5 Use the Levels and Contrast Auto Fix features to resolve common color and contrast problems.

⑤ If you like the results, click **Done**. To reject the results, click **Cancel**.

 If you prefer to adjust color settings manually, drag the Brightness and Contrast slider bars until the image is the way you want it. Picture It! defines brightness as "the amount of light that appears to emanate from a color" and contrast as "the degree of difference between the lightest and darkest parts of an image."

In addition to adjusting the brightness and contrast in your image, you can adjust the tint automatically or manually.

① Make sure the image you want to change is open in the work area.

② In the Touchup pane, choose **Adjust Tint**. The Adjust Tint task pane will open, displaying settings for Color and Amount.

③ To instruct Picture It! to adjust the tint in your image automatically, click **Tint auto fix**. Figure 5-6 displays an image whose tint was adjusted automatically.

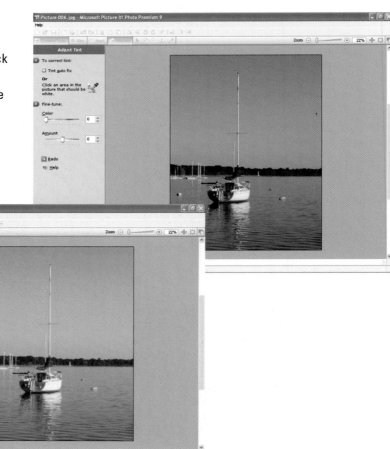

Figure 5-6 Automatically adjust the tint of an image in the Adjust Tint pane.

④ To adjust tint settings manually, drag the Color slider bar to select the color you want to change. Then drag the Amount slider bar to add more or less of the color tint.

⑤ If you like the results, click **Done**. To reject the results, click **Cancel**.

Fixing Red-Eye

Have you ever captured a perfect moment on camera, only to discover that your camera's flash turned your subject's eyes an unattractive shade of red? Fortunately, some cameras are designed to prevent red-eye in flash pictures. If your camera does not have this option, however, or if you forgot to turn it on, then you can use your image-editing program to return your photographed subject's eyes to a normal color.

Fixing Red-Eye in Photoshop Elements

To fix red-eye in Photoshop Elements, follow these steps:

1 Make sure the image you want to fix is open in the Photoshop Elements work area.

2 For more precision, click the **Zoom tool** and zoom in so the red in the eye is viewable.

 To choose the viewable area (in this case, the eye), select the Zoom tool and click and drag a box around the subject's eye.

3 Click the **Red Eye Brush tool** in the Tools palette.

4 In the options bar at the top of your screen, make sure that First Click is selected.

5 Point the brush on a red area you want to remove, and then click it (see Figure 5-7). Photoshop Elements will remove the red coloring within the circular drawing area. To use a different brush size, click the drop-down palette in the options bar in the upper-left corner of your screen.

Figure 5-7 Use Photoshop Elements' Red Eye Brush tool to remove red-eye from a picture.

Fixing Red-Eye in Picture It!

To fix red-eye in Picture It!, follow these steps:

1. Make sure the image you want to fix is open in the work area.
2. Click **Touchup** in the Common Tasks pane (if it isn't already open), and then click **Fix Red Eye**.
3. Drag the zoom slider in the Fix Red Eye toolbar to zoom in on the part of the image you want to fix.
4. Using the scroll bars in the picture work area, scroll so that you can see the red-eye.
5. Place the round pointer over the first eye and click on it.
6. Repeat Step 5 for the second eye.
7. Click **Red-eye auto fix** (see Figure 5-8).
8. Click **Done** to return to the main editing screen.

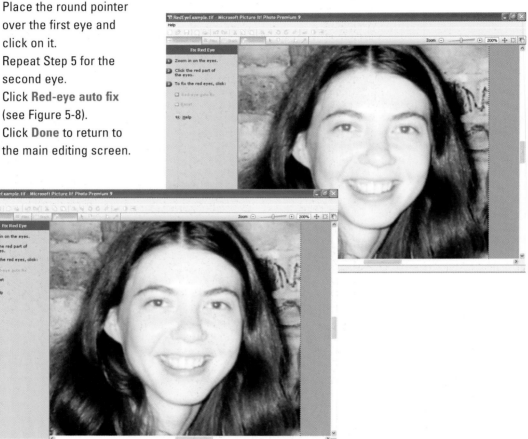

Figure 5-8 In Picture It!, use the Fix Red Eye pane to eliminate red-eye from a photograph.

Cropping an Image

If you have an out-of-place object in the background of an image, or if the subject isn't properly centered, you can cut out the unnecessary parts to better focus on your subject. Cutting out part of a picture is called cropping. As will be discussed in this section, you can use your image-editing program to crop your picture. You can even use special cutout features to create unusually shaped images, such as stars or suns.

Cropping an Image in Photoshop Elements

To crop in image in Photoshop Elements, follow these steps:

1. Make sure the image you want to crop is open in the Photoshop Elements work area.
2. Click the **Crop tool** in the Tools palette.

    Right-click the **Crop tool** to choose between a rectangular or elliptical marquee.

3. Click and drag around the part of the photograph you want to keep, as shown in the left image in Figure 5-9.
4. Click and drag the handles at the edge of the cropped area to make adjustments.
5. From the Image menu, choose **Crop**. The region surrounding the crop box will disappear, and the overall image will be resized, as shown in the right image in Figure 5-9.

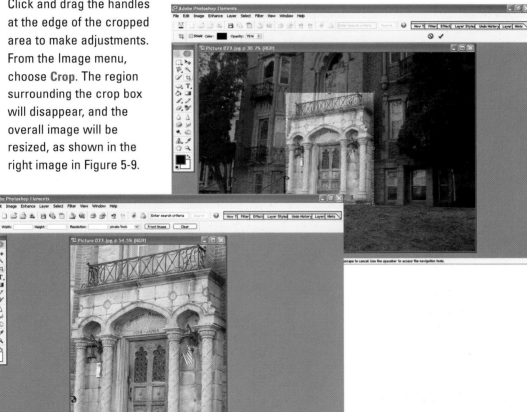

Figure 5-9 In Photoshop Elements, you can use the Crop tool to crop an image.

 The cropped image will appear smaller than the original image at first. To resize the canvas to fill the screen, choose **Fit on Screen** from the View menu.

Cropping an Image in Picture It!

To crop an image in Picture It!, follow these steps:

1. Make sure the image you want to crop is open in the Picture It! work area.
2. Click the **Format** pane in the Common Tasks pane.
3. Choose **Crop Canvas**. The Crop screen will appear.
4. Drag the resizing handles so the part of the image you want to keep is boxed. You can also drag the rotate handle to change the orientation of the cropped shape.
5. When you're ready, click **Done** to crop the picture (see Figure 5-10).

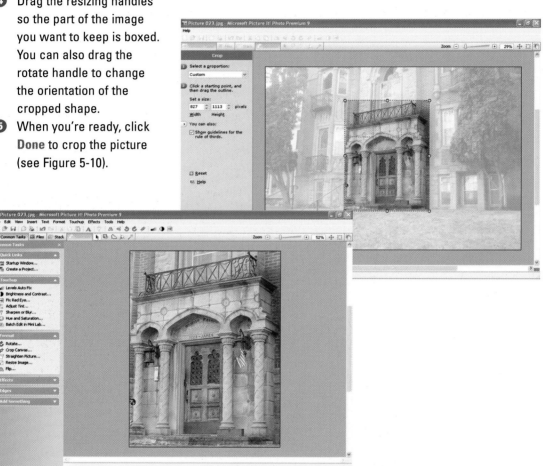

Figure 5-10 In Picture It!, use the Crop Canvas option to crop a portion of an image.

 Picture It! also enables you to crop your images using any of a series of predefined proportions. In the Crop window, select the proportion you want to use from the Select a Proportion drop-down list. (Your choices include wallet, square, and widescreen, among others.)

Rotating an Image

Sometimes digital images need to be rotated so they are displayed correctly on your monitor (for example, if you accidentally place an image upside down on the bed of your scanner). Simply use your image-editing program to rotate the image so it's displayed properly. Additionally, if a photo is slightly crooked when you scan it, you can rotate the image in your image-editing program until it is set with the proper orientation.

Rotating an Image in Photoshop Elements

To rotate an image in Photoshop Elements, follow these steps:

1 Make sure the image you want to rotate is open in the Photoshop Elements work area.

2 From the Image menu, choose **Rotate**, and then select a rotation angle (90 degrees left, 90 degrees right, or 180 degrees). Figure 5-11 shows an image rotated 90 degrees right.

3 From the Image menu, choose **Rotate**, and then **Custom** to rotate the image by a specified amount. The Rotate Canvas dialog box will appear.

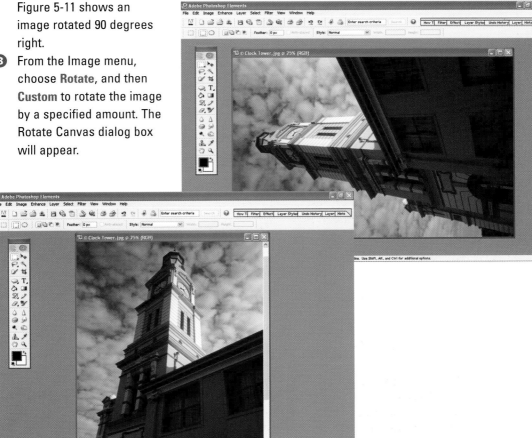

Figure 5-11 Rotate images to adjust the orientation of a photograph.

④ Enter the angle (in degrees) in the text box, and then choose whether you want to rotate the image left or right.

⑤ Click **OK**. You will return to the main work area, and the image will be rotated by the degree you specified.

⑥ After you rotate the image manually, crop it to the desired area as discussed in the previous section.

Rotating an Image in Picture It!

To rotate an image in Picture It!, follow these steps:

① Make sure the image you want to rotate is open in the Picture It! work area.

② Click the **Format** pane in the Common Tasks pane.

③ Choose **Rotate**.

④ Click the rotation you want—**Left, Half turn, Right**, or **Custom** (see Figure 5-12).

⑤ If you rotated the image manually, the edges will be slanted. To restore the orientation of the photograph, crop it to the desired area as discussed in the previous section.

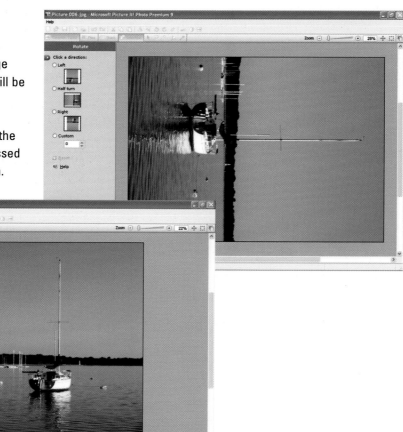

Figure 5-12 Use the Rotate window to change the orientation of a photograph in Picture It!.

Working with Cutouts

If you want to remove a selected portion of your photo, or even paste an object from one image into another, you can. Because you are essentially cutting out a region of the image, these are called cutouts. In this section, you'll learn how to create cutouts in both Photoshop Elements and Picture It!.

Adding Cutouts in Photoshop Elements

If you want, you can use a cutout to crop your image into a shape, such as a rectangle or an ellipse. Alternatively, you can create your own shape using Photoshop Elements' Magic Wand, Selection Brush, or Lasso tools. To copy a selected region of an image and paste it into another in Photoshop Elements image, follow these steps:

1. Make sure the image you want to crop is open in the Photoshop Elements work area.
2. Click the **Magic Wand tool** in the Tools palette if you want Photoshop Elements to attempt to find natural borders in the photograph and crop it automatically. Choose the **Lasso tool** if you want to draw around the area manually. Choose the **Selection Brush tool** if you want to draw over an area to select it.

    Right-click the **Lasso tool** to choose additional selection options. For example, choose Polygonal if you want to cut out a polygonal shape.

3. Use the tool you chose to select the area of the image you want to keep. Click an area with the **Magic Wand** tool, draw around a region with the **Lasso** tool, or draw over an area with the **Selection Brush** tool.

    If you use the Selection Brush tool, you can click on the brush selection drop-down palette in the options bar in the upper-left corner of your screen to select a different brush size or style.

4. From the Edit menu, choose **Copy**. This will allow you to paste the item to an existing or new image.

⑤ To paste the area, choose **Paste** from the Edit menu (see Figure 5-13).

Figure 5-13 In this example, the Selection Brush tool was used to crop the duck from the image and paste it into a new project.

 If you paste into the same image, or another image, the copied material will be superimposed over the original. Click the **Move** tool, and then click and drag the area to move it.

Adding Cutouts in Picture It!

To copy a selected region of an image and paste it into another image in Picture It!, follow these steps:

❶ Make sure the image you want to crop is open in the Picture It! work area.

❷ Click one of the selection tools from the toolbar. Click the **Magic Wand** if you want Picture It! to attempt to find natural borders in the photograph automatically. Choose the **Edge Finder** if you want to draw around the region and let Picture It! snap selection to the closest natural border. Choose the **Freehand** tool if you want to make a selection by manually drawing on the canvas.

❸ Use the tool you chose to select the area of the image you want to keep. Click on an area with the **Magic Wand**, or draw around a region with the Edge Finder or Freehand tool.

 Click the **Selection** button in the toolbar for more selection options. For example, choose to add or remove from the selection by clicking the + or – under Selection Modes, or soften the edges by choosing **Feather**.

❹ To copy the selected portion, from the Edit menu, choose **Copy**.

❺ Open the project in which you would like to paste the selection. This could be a new or existing project.

❻ To paste the area, choose **Paste** from the Edit menu (see Figure 5-14).

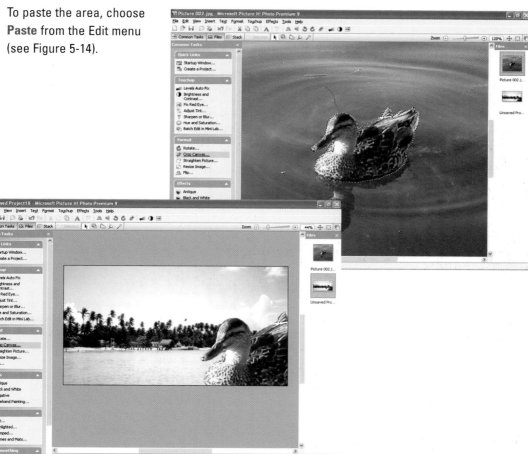

5

Figure 5-14 In this example, the Edge Finder was used to crop the duck from the image and paste it into another image.

❼ Click the image and drag to move it. Click the resize handles and drag to resize the image. Click the **Rotate** button above the image to rotate it.

Adding Special Effects

In addition to correcting problems, you can use your image-editing program to add some fun and artistic effects to your picture. For example, you can convert a color photo to black-and-white or add a sepia tone (a brownish tint) to artificially age the image. If you're feeling really funky, you can warp the picture to make it like a reflection in a funhouse mirror, turn it into a mosaic, add shadows, apply 3D effects, and much more. This section will give you a sampling of the many special effects available.

Using Color Effects

Just as you can use Photoshop Elements and Picture It! to adjust the colors in your image, you can use these programs to apply special color effects. For example, you can convert color images to black-and-white. Alternatively, you can colorize parts of your image, perhaps by creating a sepia effect or changing the color of your subject's eyes.

Applying Color Effects in Photoshop Elements

To use Photoshop Elements to colorize an image, follow these steps:

1. Make sure the image you want to colorize is open in the Photoshop Elements work area.
2. Select the **Brush** tool in the Tools palette.
3. Click the brush selection drop-down palette in the options bar (in the upper-left corner of your screen) to select a brush size or style.
4. Click the **Mode** drop-down palette in the options bar and choose **Color**.
5. In the Tools palette, click the **Set Foreground Color** box. The Color Picker dialog box will appear.
6. Select the color you want to apply to the image and click **OK**.

❼ Colorize the image by dragging the brush over it (see Figure 5-15).

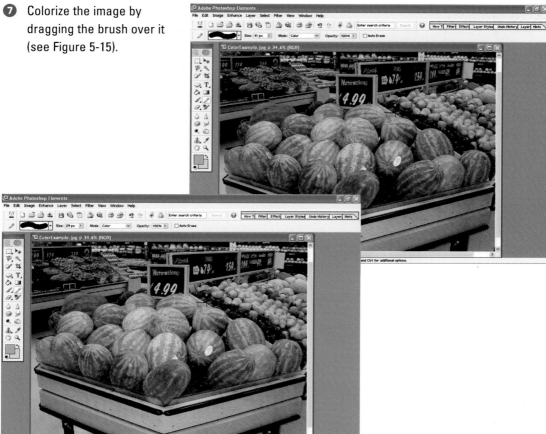

Figure 5-15 Use one of Photoshop Elements' brushes to colorize portions of a photograph.

 You can use the tools alongside the work area to zoom in, select parts of the image, and apply special effects. If you aren't sure what a particular tool does, position the mouse pointer over it, and its name will appear.

Applying Color Effects in Picture It!

To use Picture It! to convert a color image to black-and-white, follow these steps:

❶ Make sure the image you want to convert is open in the Picture It! work area.

❷ Click the **Effects** pane.

3 Click **Black and White**. The image will be converted to black-and-white (see Figure 5-16).

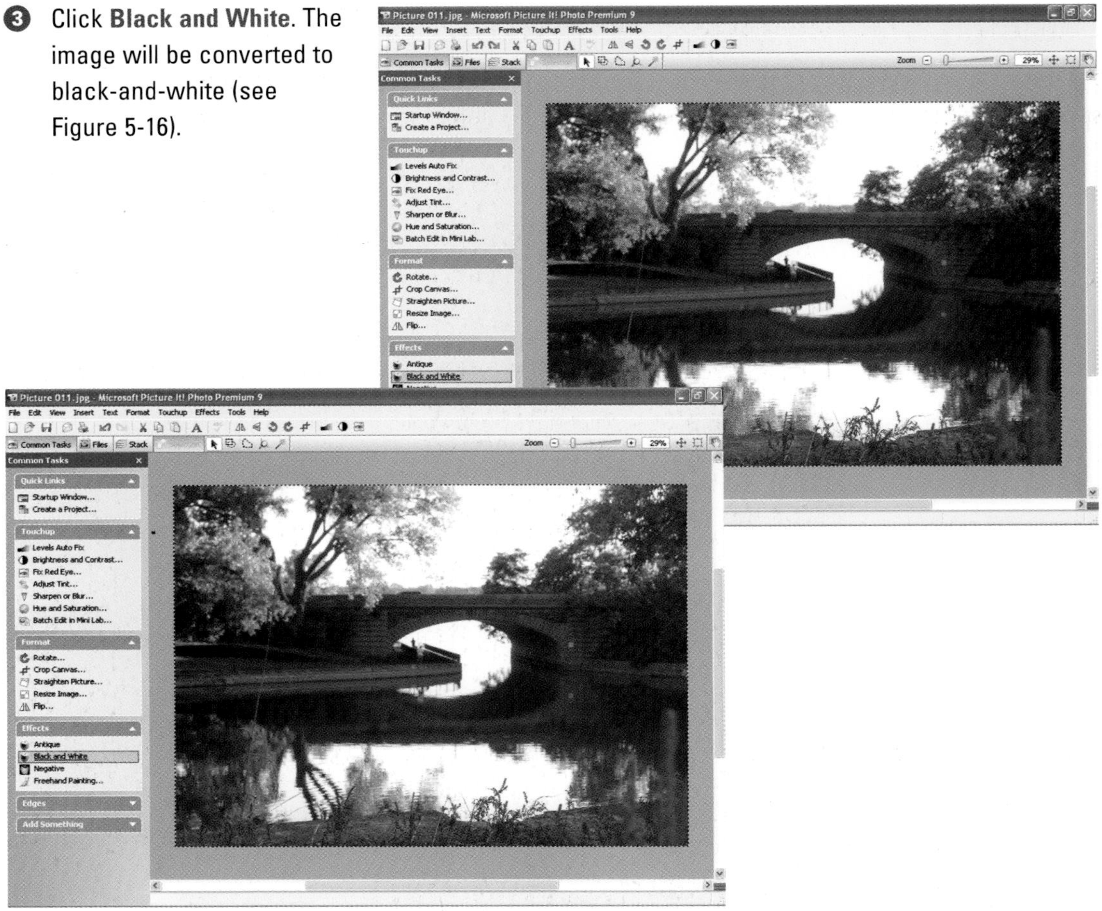

Figure 5-16 Convert a color image to black-and-white with a single click.

 The Effects pane offers other options besides Black and White, including Antique and Negative.

Adding Other Special Effects

Color effects are just the beginning of an endless variety of special effects available to you when you use an image-editing program. This section gives you a brief overview of some of the other special effects you can achieve using Photoshop Elements and Picture It!

 The best way to learn how to use these features is to experiment! Try different features to see how the results look. If you don't like the effect, simply undo your changes. (You'll learn how to undo your changes at the end of this chapter.)

Adding Special Effects in Photoshop Elements

Following are just a few of the effects you can apply using Photoshop Elements. (For specific instructions on applying these effects, consult Photoshop Elements Help.)

✦ **Apply filters.** You can use filters to apply a number of general effects to your image. You can blur the image, apply textures, and add artistic effects. To apply these special effects, choose a filter from one of the submenus in the Filters menu. Figure 5-17 shows an example of the Cutout effect from the Artistic submenu.

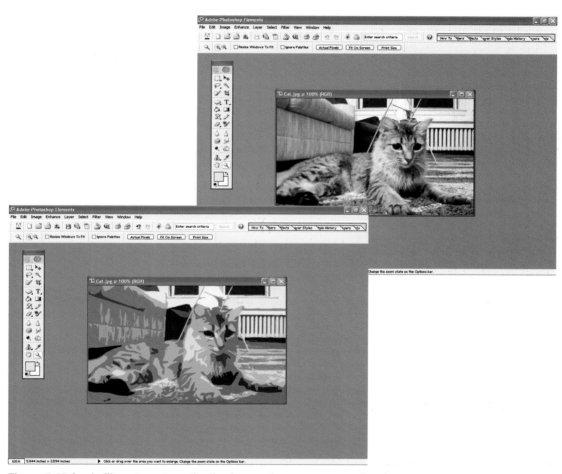

Figure 5-17 Apply filters to automatically change the appearance of an image.

✦ **Draw effects.** Draw on your image to apply colors and effects using brushes, erasers, and predefined shapes. Click the drop-down palette in the options bar (in the upper-left corner of the screen) to select a brush size or style. Then, from the Mode drop-down menu, choose one of the brush effects.

✦ **Combine photos.** Using Photoshop Elements' Photomerge option, shown in Figure 5-18, you can create panoramic sweeps. To use this feature, you need several photos that were taken while you panned the subject area.

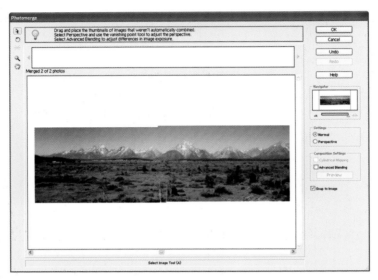

Figure 5-18 Combine photos with Photoshop Elements' Photomerge feature.

Adding Special Effects in Picture It!

Like Photoshop Elements, Picture It! offers you several options for creating special effects. You access these options through the Touchup, Photo & Color Effects, and Frame & Edge Effects menus in the Main Options task pane. Following are just a few of the available options:

✦ **Annotate your images.** Add text, clip art, or other graphic objects to your image by choosing **Add Something** in the Common Tasks pane, and then selecting the item you want to add. You can also draw on the image using different brushes.

◆ **Apply effects and filters.** You can apply several common effects to your photographs using Picture It!'s filters and effects. To select a filter, choose **Filters** from the Effects menu and select an option. Or, in the Common Tasks pane, choose **Effects**.

◆ **Use frames and edge effects.** Add polish to an image by applying frame and edge effects. Frame effects add a digital picture frame around your image, whereas edge effects change the photo's edge. You can highlight or soften the edges or apply some other effect. To change the frames or edges of your picture, click on **Edges** in the Common Tasks pane and select from the available choices.

Exploring Your Image-Editing Program

Chances are, your image-editing program features all sorts of tools to help you get the most out of your images. For example, you'll often find features designed to fix old and damaged photographs, remove dust, and sharpen the image. For specific instructions on using your image-editing program to accomplish these tasks, read the accompanying user manual or Help files. And don't be afraid to experiment! Also, as your skills in digital imaging expand, you might want to consider using an image-editing program with advanced features, such as the full version of Adobe Photoshop.

Undoing Editing Changes

Now you've done it. You've ruined a perfectly good image by adjusting its color and applying seven different special effects. What do you do?

Fortunately, if you saved your edited image as a separate file, you can scrap the edited version altogether and start over using the original, saving a new copy of it first, of course. However, if you don't want to scrap all your work, you might be able to undo just a few of your changes. Many image-editing programs have an Undo command or button you can use to undo your most recent change. In some cases, you might be able to undo multiple changes simply by clicking **Undo** multiple times.

Depending on the program you use, you might be able to undo any changes you make before you even apply them. Many programs give you the option to accept a change before you make it official. You choose whether to accept the change (thereby implementing it for good) or reject it (erasing it from your image).

 If you're ever confused about whether you've reverted to your saved image, you can always quit the program and select **No** when you are asked whether you want to save the image.

Doing More with Your Photos

Although this book provides a solid foundation for developing your skills in digital imaging, it only scratches the surface when it comes to the many options you have for producing exceptional images and the many creative things you can do with your photos. By exploring more digital camera features and the many incredible things you can do with image editing and image-management software, you can start exploiting digital photography to its fullest. In this chapter, you'll explore features that can help you take digital photography to the next level.

Enhancing Your Digital Photo Experience

Now that you've mastered the basics of digital photography, new challenges await. Your camera, computer, and digital-imaging software probably contain more gizmos and features than you'll ever need, but learning how to get acquainted with those features you do need is paramount to getting the most out of digital photography. In this section, you'll learn more about digital camera features and other resources that can help you take that next step.

Exploring Your Camera's Features

In Chapter 3, you gained some fundamental skills for taking digital photos. As you read Chapter 3, however, you probably sensed that most cameras—digital and otherwise—sport several additional features that you can use to refine your photographic technique.

Indeed, there are entire books devoted to the topic of camera technology and how you can use it to take good pictures—complete with tips and explanations about composition, special effects, lighting considerations, aperture settings, and more. See Chapter 3 for a complete discussion of these settings. Before you immerse yourself in such a book, however, try the following:

✦ **Read your camera manual.** It may not be exciting reading, but it might be the best way to learn about additional features of your camera that will help you improve your photos.

✦ **Read online or magazine articles.** There are many options available online or in magazines that describe some of the more complex photography concepts, such as f-stops and shutter speeds.

✦ **Don't be afraid to experiment!** You have nothing to lose. In fact, most of the best photographers will tell you there are no hard-and-fast rules when it comes to taking pictures. For the most part, you learn by trial and error.

✦ **If you want to specialize in a particular type of photography (such as portraits, sports photography, or nature photography), investigate the camera features that work best for that type.** For example, if your interest lies in sports photography, you'll probably want a camera with shutter-speed and lighting settings that differ from those you'd need if you planned to photograph sloths in their native habitat.

Exploring Online Options

The Internet is a great place to find more information specific to digital photography. For example, if you can't decide between two similar cameras, go online and find a review comparing the two. The Internet is also a great place to learn about the latest technology as well as time-tested techniques. Consider the following ways you can take advantage of the Internet:

✦ **Join an online photography discussion.** To share your interest with other photographers, consider joining one or several photography discussion groups (also called newsgroups or forums). In addition, you can subscribe to photography-related mailing lists, which are newsletters that are e-mailed to you periodically.

✦ **Get how-to information about craft projects.** You can go online to learn how to make buttons, posters, mugs, refrigerator magnets, calendars, family trees, T-shirts, or almost any other items that feature your favorite digital photo.

+ **Create digital stationery.** Create and send picture postcards via e-mail, or learn how to print high-quality invitations or note cards that feature your photos.

 You'll learn about the many ways to share your digital photography with others using the Internet in Chapter 8, "Sharing and Enjoying Your Images."

+ **Sell your photos.** Use an online auction site or create your own Web site to sell prints of your best photos.

+ **Learn from other photographers.** There are numerous sites on the Web dedicated to all sorts of photography subjects. Visit other photographers' Web sites to see examples of excellent photography and perhaps get a few pointers.

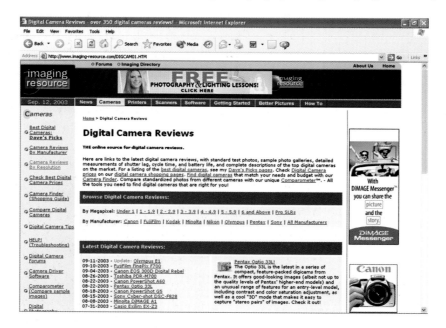

+ **Upgrade your digital-photography equipment.** As you gain experience in digital photography, you might decide you want additional equipment, such as a photo printer, special lenses, battery chargers, and so on. The Internet is a good place to look for advice and reviews, as well as to comparison-shop.

+ **Take a photography class.** Several Web sites enable you to enroll in distance-learning classes in digital photography. Distance learning is a great way for you to easily improve your skills at your own speed.

Doing More with Your Image-Editing Program

In Chapter 5, you learned the most common procedures for enhancing and manipulating digital photographs. In addition to providing many ways you can change the appearance of an image, many image-editing programs also automate other tasks. For example, when you choose a menu item, some programs launch a wizard to guide you through creating slide shows, greeting cards, calendars, Web pages, and more. In the sections that follow, you'll learn how to take advantage of several of these features and see how easy it is to do more incredible things with your photographs.

Creating Greeting Cards

Hunting for the perfect greeting card isn't always easy, and these days it's not even necessary. You can make your own professional-looking holiday cards, thank-you notes, and other greetings from home. With the help of image-editing software, you can include your own customized messages and images. To create a greeting card using Picture It!, follow these steps:

1 In Picture It!, open the picture you want to include on the greeting card.

2 In the Common Tasks pane, on the left side of your screen, under Quick Links, choose **Create a Project**.

③ Click **Cards** and then click the theme you want to use. For this example, we'll use the **Holiday** theme.

④ In the Themes pane on the left side of the screen, choose **Photo Frames**.

⑤ Click the design you want to use for your card, and then click **Open**.

 Although Picture It! displays several designs, some may not be installed on your computer. If you select a design that isn't installed, Picture It! will prompt you to insert one of the program installation discs. Insert the disc and click **Retry**.

⑥ Drag the image from the Files palette on the right side of your screen into the middle of the picture frame. The picture snaps to the middle of the frame as shown in Figure 6-1. Click **Next**.

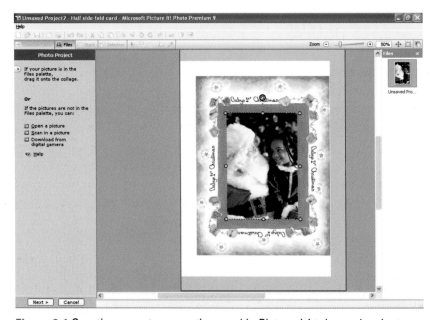

Figure 6-1 Creating a custom greeting card in Picture It! takes only minutes.

⑦ Now, you can click the corner handles and drag to resize the image. Or, click the image and drag to move it. When the image is sized and positioned, click **Done**. The card appears in the main work area.

⑧ You can view the inside spread of the card or the back by choosing from the three icons in the window to the lower left of the work area. To add text, click the **Text** tool in the toolbar at the top of the screen. Choose the font and size from the drop-down menus to the left of the Text tool. Then, type the desired text and drag it into position.

⑨ From the File menu, choose **Save** to save the card project. After printing the card, fold if necessary.

 If you need to create several copies of the same card, as you might do with a holiday card or invitation, simply choose to print multiple copies when the Print dialog box appears. You'll learn more about printing greeting cards in Chapter 7.

Creating Calendars

Creating a calendar that features your own photography can be a fun way to put your digital images to use. Personalized calendars are good for at least a year of memories and can make great gifts. You can print your calendar at home or send it to a professional for production. In this section, you'll learn how to design and produce your own custom calendar.

Creating Your Own Calendar

To create a custom calendar using Picture It!, follow these steps:

1 In Picture It!, open the pictures you want to include on the calendar.

2 In the Common Tasks pane, on the left side of your screen, under Quick Links, choose **Create a Project**.

3 Click **Calendars**, and then click the type of calendar. For this example, we'll choose **Twelve Month**.

4 Click the design you want to use for your calendar, and then click **Open**.

 If you select a design that isn't installed, Picture It! will prompt you to insert one of the program installation discs. Insert the disc and click **Retry**.

5 In the Calendar Project pane, choose the year and which day you want to begin each week. Then click **Next**.

6

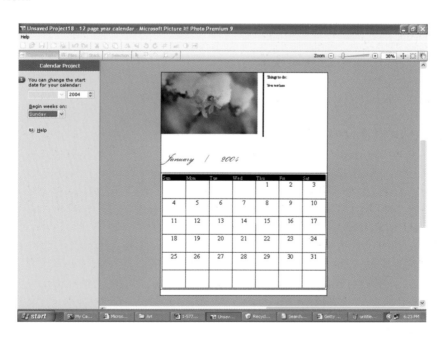

6 Drag the image from the Files palette on the right side of your screen into the photo area of the calendar (over the existing image). The picture snaps to the image frame as shown in Figure 6-2.

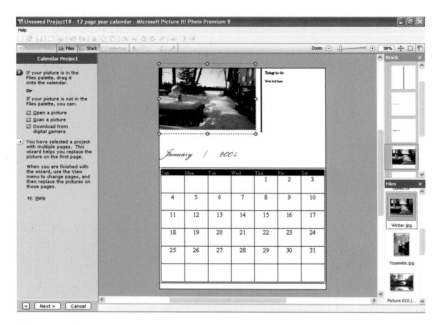

Figure 6-2 Drag an image from the Files palette to create a custom calendar with PictureIt!.

7 Click **Next**. Now, you can click the corner handles and drag to resize the image. Or, click the image and drag to move it. When the image is sized and positioned, click **Done**. The calendar appears in the main work area.

As noted in the Calendar Project pane, the wizard only guides you through placing an image on the first page of the multiple-page calendar project. To place pictures on the remaining pages, continue with these steps.

8 From the View menu, choose **Next Page** (or, in the calendar list to the lower left of the work area, click **February**). The February page of the calendar appears in the main area.

9 Click the existing image and press the **DELETE** key to remove it.

10 Drag an image from the Files palette on the right side of the screen. Then, use the handles to resize the image, and click and drag the image to move it into place. Repeat steps 8 through 10 until you have placed images on each page.

11 From the File menu, choose **Save** to save the calendar project. When the project is printed, all pages of the calendar will be sent to the printer.

After you've finished designing the calendar, you can send it to your own printer and assemble it yourself or use a professional calendar service, which you'll learn about in the next section.

Using Professional Calendar Services

If you don't want to go to the trouble, or you don't have the utilities necessary to put together your calendar, have someone do it for you. From Picture It!, you can send an electronic copy of your calendar design to a professional, who will print the calendar and send you the final product. To use a calendar service after designing a calendar with Picture It!, follow these steps:

1 Follow the steps for creating a calendar listed in the previous section.

2 With the calendar project open, from the File menu, choose **Print Professionally Online**, and then choose **Prints and Enlargements**.

3 In the Prints and Enlargements pane, choose **All pictures** on the Files palette, and then click **Next**. A screen appears giving you several print options (see Figure 6-3).

4 Click the **Order Prints** button, and follow the on-screen directions.

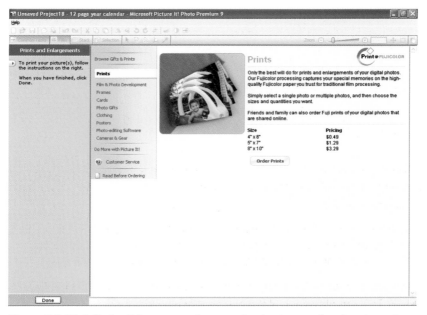

Figure 6-3 Click Order Prints to send your calendar to a professional service.

 You can also order albums, prints, and other creations using the same method.

Creating Digital Albums

Although using your computer's folder system or recordable CDs to store your digital images is practical, a more creative way to organize your images is by creating digital albums, which are much like the regular photo albums you use to store your photo prints. When you use digital photo albums, you select which pictures you want to include and arrange them in an order you choose. You'll learn how to create digital photo albums in this section. Both Picture It! and Photoshop Album include features for creating photo albums. In the following sections, you'll learn how to use these programs to accomplish this task.

Creating a Digital Album in Photoshop Album

To create an album using Photoshop Album, follow these steps:

1 In Photoshop Album, open the pictures you want to include in the album.

 As you learned in Chapter 4, you can assign tags to these photos so you can easily access the contents of this album later.

2 Hold down the **CTRL** key and click to select the photos you want to include in the album. Press **CTRL+A** to select all photos in the work area.

③ From the Creations menu, choose **Album**. The Workspace window will appear.

 You can add photos to the Workspace by dragging them from the catalog.

④ Click **Start Creations Wizard**.

⑤ Choose the album style from the list on the left and click **Next**.

⑥ Type the desired title for your album in the Title text box. Also, choose the number of photos per page and whether to include page numbers and captions. Here you can also specify a header and footer. When you've made your settings, click **Next**.

⑦ A preview of your album will appear. Use the arrow buttons to view the pages of your album. Click **Next**.

8 Choose how you want to publish your album. The options here are identical to those for publishing greeting cards and calendars. For example, Figure 6-4 shows an album saved as a PDF and opened in Acrobat Reader. These PDF files are relatively small in file size and work well for transfer over the Internet.

Figure 6-4 Albums saved as PDF files can be opened in Adobe Acrobat Reader.

 PDF files saved in an Adobe family product are compatible with additional features in Acrobat Reader. For example, you can export photos, order prints online, and more. Click **Picture Tasks** in Acrobat Reader to access these features.

Creating a Digital Album in Picture It!

To create an album using Picture It!, follow these steps:

1 In Picture It!, open the pictures you want to include in the album.

 See Chapter 5 for help opening pictures in Picture It!.

2 In the Quick Links section of the Common Tasks pane, click **Create a Project**.

3 Click **Albums**.

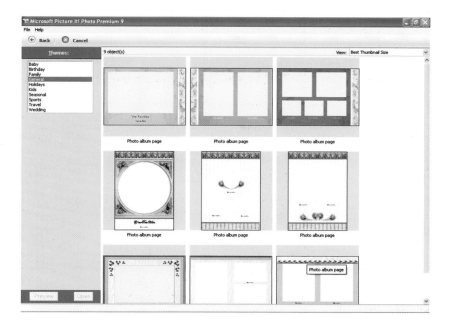

4 Click **Album Sets** to view a list of design options for your album pages, including background images and placeholders for pictures. From the list on the left, you can choose from several designs or themes, including Baby, Birthday, Family, General, Kids, Travel, Wedding, Holiday, seasonal, and Sports.

5 Click a design that relates to the photographs you want to include, and then click **Open**.

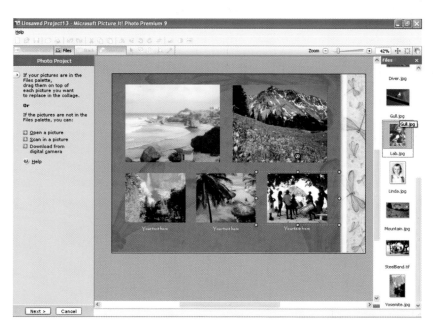

Although Picture It! displays several designs, some may not be installed on your computer. If you select a design that isn't installed, Picture It! will prompt you to insert one of the program installation discs. Insert the disc and click **Retry**.

6 Drag a picture from the Files palette on the right side of your screen to a placeholder on the album page.

 If you discover that you forgot to open a picture you want to include in your album, click **Open a Picture** and add it.

7 Drag a sizing handle to move or resize your image as needed. You also can flip images horizontally or vertically. (Refer to Chapter 5 for additional information on this action.)

8 Repeat steps 6 and 7 for all placeholders on the page. When you're finished, click **Next**.

9 Click **Next**, and then click **Done**. The album will appear in Picture It!'s main editor window, as shown in Figure 6-5.

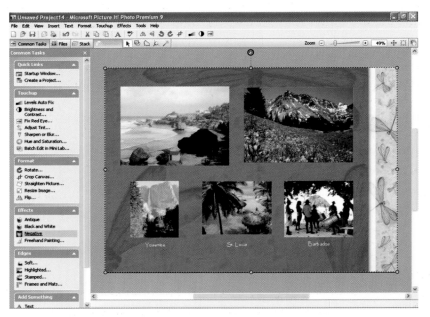

Figure 6-5 Create your own digital photo albums in Picture It!.

10 If the album page includes any text placeholders, delete the text and replace it with your own.

11 Click **File** and then click **Save As**. Navigate to the folder where you want the album stored and give it a descriptive name.

After you've saved your album, you can add pages to it by repeating the steps just listed. When your album is complete, you can print it. (Refer to Chapter 7 for more information about printing.)

> ### More About... Picture It! Designs
>
> An album is only one of the projects you can complete using Picture It! Others include business cards, crafts, envelopes, papers, and collages. To experiment with these options, choose **Create a Project** from the File menu or click **Create a Project** in the Common Tasks pane. For more information, consult Picture It! Help.

Creating Digital Slide Shows

Another way to showcase your pictures is to create a digital slide show. In a slide show, the images are displayed full-screen on your computer, one after another. You can create a slide show of your images using Windows XP or your image-editing program.

 A slide show is a great way to broadcast your photos over the Internet or share them via e-mail. Chapter 8 covers the specifics of displaying digital photographs online.

Creating a Slide Show in Windows XP

To create a slide show using Windows XP, follow these steps:

1 Place all the photos you want to include in one folder within the My Pictures folder.

 To ensure you can access the slide show option in Windows XP, place photo files in the My Pictures folder or one of its subfolders.

2 Open the folder that contains the pictures.

3 In the task pane on the left side of the window, click **View as a slide show**. Windows XP will display all the images in full-screen mode in a continuously running slide show.

④ Move the mouse pointer to the upper-right corner of the screen. A row of control buttons will appear, as shown in Figure 6-6. Play the slide show, move through the photos, or close the slide show by clicking the appropriate button.

Figure 6-6 Create your own digital slide shows in Windows XP.

Projects for Kids

Image-editing software makes many fun projects possible for children of all ages. From scanning an artistic masterpiece and sending it to Grandma to creating trading cards and collages, all you need is a computer and a little imagination. In addition, bringing digital-imaging technology into book reports and other projects can be an easy and fun way to impress your fourth-grade English teacher. In this section, you'll explore some inventive ways to create your own works of art using digital images and features found in most image-editing software (no Ph.D. required).

Digital Collages

Using image-editing software, you can combine a number of images to create a collage. You can incorporate several full pictures or you can crop, copy, and paste portions of pictures into a single collage. To create a collage in Picture It!, follow these steps:

 To create a collage using one of Picture It!'s frame designs, click **Create a Project** in the Quick Links section of the Common Tasks pane. Choose **Albums**, and then choose **Collages**. Then follow the instructions for creating a digital album in Picture It! (explained earlier in the chapter).

1 First, open the file you want to act as the background. From the File menu, choose **Open**.

2 Locate and double-click an image to open it.

 To start a new document for the collage, from the File menu, choose **New**. Then adjust the canvas size in the upper-left portion of the screen and click **Done**.

3 From the Insert menu, choose **Picture**, and then select **From My Computer**.

4 Locate the picture you want to add, and then double-click to open it. The picture will appear over the existing image. Click anywhere on the image and drag to move it so you can see one of the corners (if you can't already).

5 Now click the corner of the image and drag to resize it. Click the middle of the image and drag it to position it.

6 You can use the **Rotate** button above the image to rotate the image, as shown in Figure 6-7.

Figure 6-7 Create collages of your favorite images by inserting them into an existing project.

7 To add text to your collage, click the **Text** tool in the tool palette, choose the font and size from the drop-down menus at the top of your screen, and then double-click and start typing.

Trading Cards

You can create your own custom trading cards using Picture It!. To do so, follow these steps:

1 In Picture It!, open the picture you want to place on the trading card.

2 In the Quick Links section of the Common Tasks pane, click **Create a Project**.

3 Click **Photo Crafts**, and then click **Trading Cards**.

4 Click the **theme** you want to use, and then click **Open**.

 Remember, if you select a design that isn't installed, Picture It! will prompt you to insert one of the program installation discs. Insert the disc and click **Retry**.

5 Drag a picture from the Files palette on the right side of your screen to a placeholder on the trading card page.

6 Drag a sizing handle to move or resize the image as needed. You can also flip images horizontally or vertically. (Refer to Chapter 5 for additional information on this action.)

7 Click **Next**, and then click **Done**. The trading card will appear in Picture It!'s main editor window.

8 Replace the text placeholders. Double-click to display the insertion point, and then delete the existing text and replace it with your own, as shown in Figure 6-8.

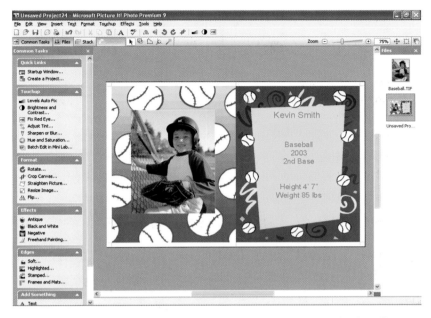

Figure 6-8 Use Picture It! to create trading cards with customized trading card and text.

9 Click **File** and then click **Save As**. Navigate to the folder where you want to store the trading card, and then give it a descriptive name.

Reports and Papers

If you're using Microsoft Word or another common word processing program for a book report or another assignment, adding a digital image is easy. Just follow these steps:

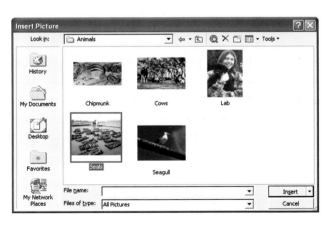

1 Move the cursor where you would like to place the image.

2 From the Insert menu, choose **Picture**, and then choose **From File**. The Insert Picture dialog box will appear.

③ Navigate to the picture you want to add, and then double-click it. The picture will appear in the word processing document, as shown in Figure 6-9.

Figure 6-9 Insert digital images into word processing documents to enhance homework assignments and school projects.

After inserting an image, click it to activate the resize handles. Click a handle and drag to resize the image.

 Most word processing programs, such as Word, also contain a collection of clip art, including a variety of illustrations and pictures. To add clip art to your document, from the Insert menu, choose **Picture** and then **Clip Art**.

Saving Artwork on Your Computer

You can do much more with your scanner than simply transfer photographs and documents. Now you can scan and archive on your computer your paintings, drawings, or other two-dimensional artwork, as shown in Figure 6-10. Simply scan the artwork as you would a photograph (as described in Chapter 4). After you have saved your masterpiece as a digital image, you can print a copy, edit it using image-editing software, or e-mail it to Grandma. You'll learn more about e-mailing digital images in Chapter 8.

Figure 6-10 Scan artwork to store it on your computer, or send it to a printer to make copies.

Printing Your Images

You've used a digital camera or scanner to obtain digital images and a photo-editing program to touch them up. Now you're ready to share your pictures with your friends and family. This chapter covers the more traditional way of sharing photographs—by making prints.

When it comes to printing digital images, you have many options depending on your equipment and the quality you want. You can print your pictures using a regular printer or a special photo printer. Alternatively, you can take your digital picture files to a local photo store or send them to an online printing service and have regular prints made. Read on to learn the specifics of all these options.

Using Your Printer

One of the fastest and easiest ways to print a digital image is to use your printer, whether it's a regular document printer or a special photo printer. This section discusses both types of printers, outlines some considerations for getting the highest-quality printouts, and walks you through the process of printing your images.

Using a Standard Printer

If price and convenience are your primary considerations, you can print photographs using your regular document printer. Although you probably won't get professional-quality prints using this type of printer, you can find many uses for the prints you create with it, such as in reports, family newsletters, informal invitations, and more.

If you're using your regular printer to print your digital images, keep the following points in mind:

- To print color pictures, you must have a color printer. If your printer is black and white, your color pictures will print in shades of gray.

- The quality of a printer's printout (the resolution) is measured in dots per inch (dpi). The more dots per inch, the finer the image. If you have a low-resolution printer (in the 300 dpi range), your printed pictures might look grainy—that is, the dots that make up the image may be visible.

- Although regular printers are less capable of reproducing all of the precision changes made with your image-editing software, you can still crop, rotate, fix red-eye, and otherwise adjust your images before printing.

- For better-quality photo prints, try printing on special photo paper and using the correct ink. (See the "Choosing the Best Paper and Ink" section later in this chapter for details.)

Using a Special Photo Printer

If you want to create print-shop quality printouts of your images in the comfort of your own home or business, consider investing in a special photo printer. Photo printers offer several benefits, including the following:

- **Convenience.** Instead of taking your image files to a regular photo lab or ordering prints online, you can print high-quality photographs right from your desktop with the click of a button.

- **Quality.** With photo-quality paper, you can use a photo printer to create photo-shop quality prints.

- **No computer needed.** Most photo printers can print directly from a digital camera or memory card, which means you don't need your PC to make prints.

- **Portability.** The portability of photo printers comes in handy any time you attend a family reunion or other event. You can take pictures with your digital camera and print your images on the spot to share with the rest of the family.

◆ **Small footprint.** The footprint refers to the space a component takes up on a desk or other work area. Most photo printers leave a small footprint, meaning they are fairly small.

Photo printers are available at your local computer or electronics store and online. They come in a wide range of models, from the simple to the sophisticated. Of course, you can expect to pay more for higher-quality printers.

If you're thinking about buying a photo printer, you need to decide what type of printer best suits your needs. As you research and compare the many photo printers on the market, ask these questions:

◆ **Does the printer have to be attached to your computer to print?** Some printers must be attached to the computer in order to print, whereas others print directly from your digital camera or the digital camera memory card. If you want to use your printer while on the go, you'll be well served by a printer that can print directly from your camera or memory card.

◆ **How is the printer attached?** If the printer attaches to your computer, does it attach via a standard LPT (Line Printer) or parallel port, via a serial port, or via a USB port?

◆ **What type of media can the printer read?** If your camera has removable media, make sure that the photo printer can read the type of media the camera uses. For example, if your camera uses SmartMedia cards, make sure the printer is compatible with them.

◆ **What size prints can you produce?** Most low-end photo printers can print only 4×6 prints, the size offered by most photo labs. If you want larger images, check the available print sizes for that printer.

◆ **How fast is the printer?** Some printers measure print speed as the time it takes to print a picture, while others measure it in pages per minute (ppm). You can find printers in the range of 12 to 15 ppm for black and white and 10 to 12 ppm for color.

◆ **What is the quality of the printout?** Quality, also called resolution, is measured in dots per inch (dpi). 2400×1200 dpi is common.

The best way to compare printout quality is to visit a computer-supply store and view the actual printouts from various printers. Otherwise, all the detailed specifications in the world won't help you choose.

◆ **What supplies do you need?** The component used when printing photos is the ink your printer uses, not to mention the special photo paper you need for high-quality prints. Different printers use different types of ink and paper; compare these items as well before choosing a printer.

◆ **What software is included with the printer?** Some printers come bundled with graphics software, and virtually all include the required drivers.

◆ **What are the system requirements for the printer?** Just as your PC must meet minimum system requirements to work with your digital camera or scanner, it also must meet system requirements to work with a photo printer. Before you buy a particular printer, be sure your system makes the grade.

◆ **What other equipment do you need?** If a printer cable is not included with the photo printer, you will need to purchase one separately.

If you don't have a regular document printer, you might consider purchasing a printer that can handle both documents and photos.

Getting the Best Prints

Whether you use a document printer or a photo printer, you can make sure you get the best possible prints by correctly sizing the image, choosing the best paper and ink, and using the right printer settings.

Sizing the Image

Because most computer monitors display graphics at 72 dpi, most image-editing programs display image files at the same resolution, regardless of the resolution setting you used when you took the picture. If you chose a high-resolution setting, the digital image will simply appear larger on your PC's desktop (sometimes the size of a regular piece of paper). Low-resolution images, on the other hand, will appear smaller because they contain fewer pixels than high-resolution images (see Figure 7-1).

100 dpi   200 dpi   300 dpi

Figure 7-1 Higher-resolution images contain more pixels and greater detail.

However, chances are you usually will want your printed images to be smaller than they appear on your monitor at 72 dpi. For one thing, even high-resolution images appear grainy if they're too large. For another, it's hard to fit an 8×10 photo of your dog into your wallet. Fortunately, most photo programs let you specify how large you want your printed photo to be in inches; options typically include 3.5×5, 4×6, 5×7, and so on. This doesn't change the number of pixels your photo contains; rather, it changes the amount of space those pixels occupy in inches.

 If your digital image is shaped oddly—that is, it won't quite fit into one of the available size options—your photo program might use a resizing algorithm to add or subtract pixels as needed.

Choosing the Best Paper and Ink

Regular paper is coarse and absorbs ink, often smearing the dots that make up a digital picture on an inkjet printer. Photo paper, on the other hand, is coated, and this coating prevents ink from soaking into the paper. The result is crisp dots and, thus, a clearer picture. For even better results, you can use special ink that dries quickly to prevent smearing.

To determine the type of ink and paper you should use, check the documentation for your particular printer. Practically every printer manufacturer sells paper and ink designed to work with their various printers. It's usually best to stick with your printer manufacturer's line of products, but some third-party paper and ink products may provide adequate quality.

Using the Correct Printer Settings

To obtain the best possible photo prints using your regular printer or a photo printer, you'll probably need to adjust various print settings, such as paper type, print quality, and print mode. Available settings vary from printer to printer, but you can check your printer's settings by following these steps:

 Changing a printer's settings affects all jobs you perform using that printer. Changing your regular printer's settings to handle digital photos might adversely affect the way in which regular documents are printed. To avoid this problem, you can usually change printer settings as you print, whether you do so using Windows XP or your photo-editing program. You'll learn how in the next section.

7

1. Click start, and then click Control Panel.
2. Click Printers and Other Hardware.
3. Click View installed printers or fax printers. A list of all installed printers will appear.
4. Right-click the printer you're using. A shortcut menu will appear; click Printing Preferences.

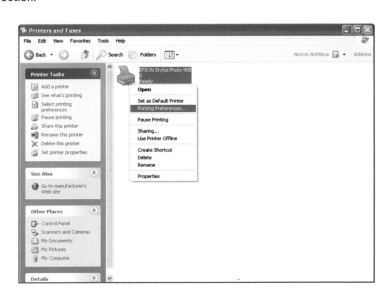

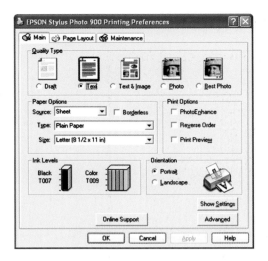

⑤ The Printing Preferences dialog box for the printer you selected will open. Here you can control the level of quality for the print job, choose the paper type and orientation, and adjust other settings. Make changes as needed and click OK.

 Your Printing Preferences dialog box might look different from the one shown here. For help with the available settings, consult your printer's manual or click Help (question mark button) in the upper-right corner of the Printing Preferences dialog box.

Printing Pictures

You've decided what type of printer you want to use, you've properly sized your image, you've bought the correct paper and ink, and you've configured your printer to best handle printing digital images. At last it's time to print your images! You can do so using Windows XP's Photo Printing Wizard or your photo-editing program's print feature. The following sections cover printing from Windows XP, Photoshop Elements, and Picture It!.

Printing Pictures from Windows XP

To print pictures using Windows XP, follow these steps:

① Select start, and then click My Computer.

② Open the folder or subfolder that contains the image files you want to print.

 Windows XP provides a My Pictures folder within the My Documents folder, in which you can store all your image files. Using this folder consistently ensures quick and easy file retrieval. For more information about organizing photos, see Chapter 4.

③ Click **Print pictures** in the Picture Tasks pane, as shown in Figure 7-2.

Print pictures

Figure 7-2 You can print pictures directly from your My Pictures folder.

④ The Photo Printing Wizard will start, displaying its Welcome screen. Click **Next**.

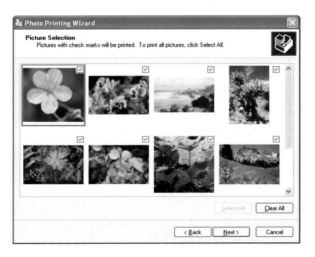

⑤ The Wizard will display a screen containing thumbnail images of all the digital pictures in the folder. To print all of them, click **Select All**. If you want to print only some of them, click the check boxes above the ones you want to print. When you've selected all the pictures you want to print, click **Next**.

If you accidentally select an image that you don't want to print, simply click in its check box to deselect it. To deselect all images at once, click Clear All.

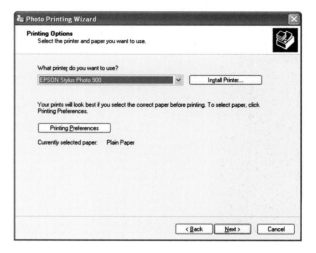

6 Windows will prompt you to select the printer you want to use. If the correct printer isn't displayed by default, click the down-arrow next to the default printer and select the correct one from the list.

 If the printer you want to use doesn't appear in the list, it hasn't been installed yet on your PC. To install it, click Install Printer and follow the instructions Windows XP issues.

7 Click Next. The Wizard's Layout Selection screen will appear, enabling you to select the size and layout of your pictures and preview your selection. Review the choices in the Available Layouts section of the dialog box; when you find a size and layout you like, click it. Your layout choice will be highlighted.

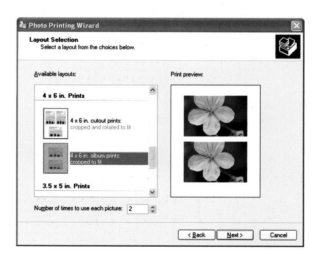

8 Specify how many times each picture should be printed. For example, to print two 4×6 album copies of each picture, click 4×6 in. album prints: cropped to fit in the Available layouts section, and then use the spin arrows or enter 2 in the Number of times to use each picture spin box. Click Next.

If you change your mind about a selection you've made in one of the Wizard screens, click Back to step backward through the Wizard until you locate the screen containing the setting you want to change. Change the setting as needed, and then click Next to continue.

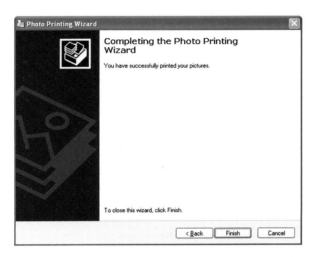

⑨ The pictures will be printed, and the Wizard's final screen will open. Click Finish to close the Wizard.

More About . . . Windows XP Features

Using Windows XP, you can set up accounts for multiple users, and each user can customize many of the features of Windows, such as the desktop. Also, each person with an XP account has a My Documents folder with a My Pictures folder.

If you are working on a computer with more than one user account, you will see the pictures in your account's My Pictures folder. To access pictures in another user's My Pictures folder, you need to log out and then log in as that user. You can also choose to share a folder with other users of the same computer or even other computers over a network. To share a folder's contents with other users, right-click the folder and choose Sharing and Security. Select the users you want to grant access to the folder and click OK.

Printing Pictures from Photoshop Elements

To print pictures using Photoshop Elements, follow these steps:

❶ Open the picture you want to print in the Photoshop Elements work area.

 If you need help opening image files in Photoshop Elements, refer to Chapter 5.

② Click **Print Preview**. The Print Preview dialog box will appear. Before you change these settings, you'll need to establish the page size and orientation.

③ Click **Page Setup**. The Page Setup dialog box will appear, as shown in Figure 7-3.

Figure 7-3 Select the orientation and page size in the Page Setup dialog box.

 To select the printer you want to use, click **Printer** in the Page Setup dialog box. Choose the desired printer and click **OK**.

④ In the Page Setup dialog box, you can select the orientation (portrait or landscape) and choose the paper size. Adjust these settings as needed, and then click **OK**. You will return to the Print Preview dialog box, as shown in Figure 7-4.

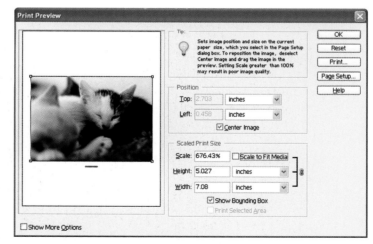

Figure 7-4 Preview and adjust the placement and size of the image in the Print Preview dialog box.

⑤ In the left side of the Print Preview dialog box, you can click the resize handles to change the size of the picture. To move the image, uncheck Center Image and drag the image in the preview area. Use options on the right side of the dialog box to make additional positioning and sizing adjustments. When you've adjusted the settings as desired, click Print. The Print dialog box will appear.

⑥ In the Print dialog box, specify the number of copies, and then click OK to begin printing.

 Click the Properties button in the Print dialog box to adjust additional printer settings or change the printer. If you change printer settings as you print, you don't change the way regular documents are printed.

Printing Pictures from Picture It!

To print pictures using Picture It!, follow these steps:

① Open the picture you want to print so it appears in the main work area.

 If you need help opening image files in Picture It!, refer to Chapter 5.

② Click the Print button on the toolbar at the top of your screen. The Print pane will appear on the left side of your screen containing a variety of options, as shown in Figure 7-5.

Figure 7-5 Configure print settings in the Print pane.

❸ Notice there are three steps listed in the Print pane. First, select the printer and number of copies. Next, choose the print size. Finally, select the orientation. When you've made your selections, click Print. The image will be sent to the printer.

 If you plan to print using paper other than standard paper, be sure to insert the correct paper type in your printer before you print the image.

More About... Printing Multiple Pictures

Using Picture It!, you can print several photos at once. To do so, first open all the photos you want to print. Click the Print button to open the Print task pane, and then click Print multiple pictures or special paper. In the Print Layout task pane that appears, you can choose to print one picture per page or several pictures on each page; click the appropriate box to select it. Then, in the Print task pane, select the printer to be used, the paper orientation (landscape or portrait), and the print size, and then click Next. Drag pictures from the Files palette on the right side of your screen to the appropriate area, and then click Next. Finally, choose the number of copies you want to print, and then click Print to print the pictures.

Printing Projects—Greeting Cards, CDs, and More

With the ever-increasing capability of desktop printers, projects that required professional printing in the past can now be done at home. For example, you can use a photo printer to print your digital images on greeting cards. Some printers can even print directly onto a CD. In this section, you'll learn how to accomplish both of these tasks.

Printing Greeting Cards

You can print greeting cards with any printer. All that's required is a software program that guides you through the creation process. In Chapter 6, you learned to create greeting cards using image-editing programs. However, if you don't own image-editing software, you might be relieved to know that software designed to create projects such as greeting cards often comes bundled with your printer. For example, Epson's Film Factory, shown in Figure 7-6, guides you through creating a variety of projects.

Figure 7-6 You can use Epson's Film Factory, which accompanies Epson printers, to manage photos and create a variety of projects.

To print a greeting card using Film Factory, follow these steps:

1. Open the picture you want to print so it appears in the main work area. To import a photo into the work area, click Import on the toolbar at the top and choose From File.

2. Then, locate the file you want to open and click Copy. The image will appear in Film Factory's main work area.

3. In the Print Options pane on the left side of your screen, choose Greeting Cards. The Greeting Cards pane will appear on the left side of your screen with four steps for creating the card.

④ Click to select the photo you want to place on the greeting card, and then click Step 2: Choose Layout.

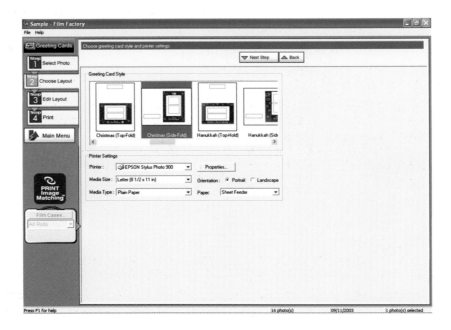

⑤ Use the scroll bar to browse through available greeting card styles and click the one you want to use. You can also select the page size, orientation, and paper type here. When you've adjusted your settings as desired, click Step 3: Edit Layout.

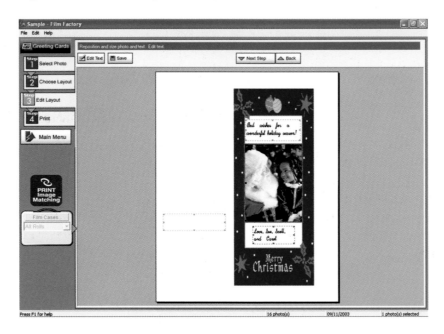

⑥ Click and drag the photo to move it.

⑦ Click one of the corner image handles and drag to resize the image.

⑧ Double-click one of the text boxes to open the Edit Text dialog box, in which you can add text.

⑨ When you've finished making layout changes and adding text, click Step 4: Print.

⑩ Choose the number of copies. If you'd like to change additional printer settings, click the Properties button.

⑪ When you're ready to print, click the Print button. The greeting card is sent to the printer.

 Some greeting card layouts require you to fold the printed page into a fold-out card. To do this, you generally need to hold the page so the image on the front of the card appears on the lower-right side of the page, and the interior portion appears upside-down on the upper-left side of the page. Fold the top half back, and then fold the left side back to complete the fold-out card.

Printing CDs

Printers are capable of printing far more than documents, photos, and greeting cards. In fact, some printers, such as the Epson Photo Stylus, can even print images and text directly to printable CDs and DVDs. For example, after burning a slide show onto a CD-R, you can print a custom label directly onto the CD's printable surface. CD-printing software is usually straightforward and easy to use. For example, to print to a CD or DVD using Epson's Print CD software, follow these steps:

 If you plan to print to a CD-R, save images or other data to the CD-R before you print the label.

① Open Print CD. A new blank template will appear on the screen. For this example, you'll add a digital photo and text to a CD label design.

② From the Import menu, choose Picture. The Select Picture dialog box will appear.

③ Click the File tab and then click Browse. Locate the folder containing the image you want to add and click OK.

④ Click the file you want to use and click OK. The image will appear in Print CD's main window.

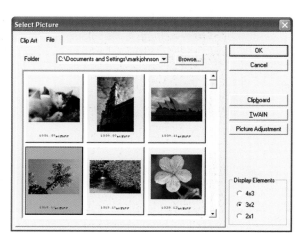

⑤ Click the image to move it or use the handles to resize the image so the portion you want to include on the CD appears within the CD boundaries, as shown in Figure 7-7.

Figure 7-7 In Epson's Print CD software, resize and move the image so it appears within the CD boundaries.

⑥ To add text, click the **Text** button on the left side of your screen. The Text Settings dialog box will appear.

7 In the Text Settings dialog box, type the text. To change the font, size, or style, choose the Text Settings tab. You can arc text to the contour of the CD by choosing Auto Arc under the Text tab. When you've adjusted your settings, click OK.

8 Place the printable CD on your printer's CD tray. Check your printer's manual to ensure the CD is placed correctly.

9 Click the Print icon on the toolbar at the top of your screen. The Print dialog box will appear. You can confirm the number of copies and adjust other print settings.

10 Click OK to send the image to the printer.

 CD-labeling software also usually includes formats for jewel case labels and inserts.

Other Printing Projects

Film Factory and other print-oriented programs offer printing options not available in image-editing software. For example, with Film Factory, it's easy to add borders and crop marks and specify a combination of print sizes on the same page, as shown in Figure 7-8. You can also create duplicate prints, index prints (with many photos on a page), and sticker prints.

 Although printing software is a great way to manage images for printing, it's usually not the best choice for image editing. Dedicated image-editing programs, such as Photoshop Elements and Picture It!, are the preferred choice for touching up and editing your photos.

Figure 7-8 Use printing programs such as Film Factory to place different-sized prints on the same page and perform other print-specific tasks.

Printing at Your Local Photo Lab

Suppose you've tried printing your images using your regular printer, but you decide you want enlargements or print-shop quality pictures. One option is to purchase a photo printer. But as another option, you can have your digital images printed at your local photo lab—at a price comparable to that of film-based photo processing.

Many photo labs have self-service photo-processing kiosks, into which you can insert your camera's removable media card, for example, a SmartMedia or CompactFlash card, and then print pictures directly from the card. Alternatively, the photo lab might be able to print the images on your media card for you.

To find a reliable photo lab that processes digital prints, start with the lab you use to develop your film-based prints. Ask whether they offer digital-print processing and, if so, how it works. If your local lab doesn't provide this service, try other photo labs or drugstores.

In addition to enabling you to print photographs taken with your digital camera, many photo labs can convert photographs taken with a film-based camera into digital images. When you drop off your roll of film, you simply specify that you want your images to be digitized in addition to being printed; depending on your selection, these digital images are then stored on a CD-ROM or on the Web. You can copy these images to your computer and then manipulate, edit, and e-mail them just as you would with digital images you obtained using your scanner or digital camera.

Using an Online Printing Service

If your local photo lab can't handle your digital media, don't despair. You can use one of the many online services to print your digital pictures. You simply upload the pictures from your computer to the online printing service's computer, and the online service will print the photos and mail them to you. Most of these services will also post them to a

Web page for you to view. Of course, these services can't offer the one-hour turnaround time found at many photo labs, but you can expect to receive your photos within a few days.

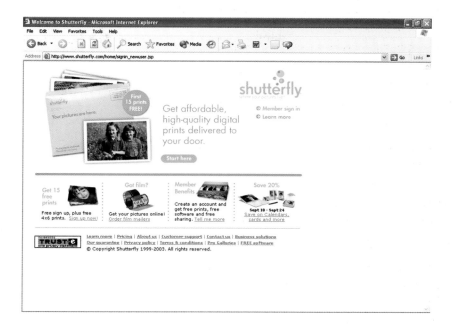

Turnaround time aside, online printing offers many benefits.

✦ **You can order copies of only the pictures you want.** Instead of developing an entire "roll," many online printing services will post digital copies of your prints to a Web site for you to preview. That way you can decide which pictures you want printed.

✦ **You can order prints in various sizes.** These include traditional photo-print sizes (3.5×5 and 4×6), enlargements (5×7 and 8×10), and smaller sizes, such as wallet prints.

✦ **You can order multiple copies of prints you like.** If you've ever ordered double prints when you've had regular film processed, you've probably ended up with extra copies of prints you don't like. When you process your digital prints using an online service, however, you can order one or more prints of any you like by viewing them online and choosing which ones you want to order right from your own computer. You can also order many kinds of photo gifts such as cards, mugs, and even framed prints from most of these services and have them delivered right to your home.

Online print services charge about as much as a typical photo lab, although you also must pay for shipping and handling. Some online print services, however, have introductory offers that enable you to receive several free prints so you can check their quality. Only after you've used all your free prints do you pay for processing.

 In case you're not satisfied with any prints, most print services provide a guarantee: You can return the prints for credit if they don't meet your expectations.

One way to access an online printing service is to type its URL in your Web browser's Address field. You can then follow the site's directions to upload your image files. Be sure to check out the site's printing and shipping charges and turnaround time first.

If you'd rather not hunt down an online print service on your own, you can use Windows XP or your photo-editing program to connect to one. The following sections cover using Windows XP, Photoshop Elements, and PictureIt! to order prints online.

 You must be logged on to the Internet to order prints online.

Using Windows XP to Order Prints Online

To order prints online using Windows XP, you use the Online Print Ordering Wizard. Here's how:

❶ In My Computer, open the folder or subfolder that contains the image files you want to print.

② Click Order prints online in the Picture Tasks pane.

③ The Online Print Ordering Wizard will start, displaying its Welcome screen. Click Next.

④ The Wizard will display a screen containing thumbnail images of all the digital pictures in the folder. To upload all of them to the online print service, click Select All. If you want to upload only some of them, click the check boxes above the ones you want to upload. When you've selected all the pictures you want to upload, click Next.

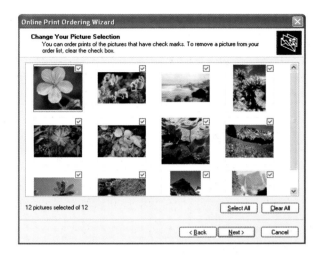

 If you accidentally select an image that you don't want to upload, simply click its check box to deselect it. To deselect all images at once, click Clear All.

⑤ The Online Print Ordering Wizard will display a list of online print services. Choose the one you want to use, and then click Next.

⑥ Some online print services prompt you to set up a Microsoft .NET Passport account. To do so, simply follow the steps in the .NET Passport Wizard (which opens automatically) and click Next to move from screen to screen. You'll be prompted to provide your e-mail address, a password, and information about your location (country, state, and ZIP code).

⑦ Depending on the print service you select, you might be prompted to set up an account with the service. This process is similar to registering for a .NET Passport account; you enter your e-mail address, password, and name.

⑧ When you're logged on to the photo service's Web site, follow the onscreen instructions to order your prints.

7

More About . . . Ordering Prints Online

The precise instructions for uploading image files and setting print options vary depending on which service you use, but a few things are constant. For example, you can expect to select a size and quantity as well as review pricing information for each print. Also, you'll need to enter shipping and billing information. When that's done, you upload your picture files from your computer to the printing service. (Depending on your connection speed, this can take a while.) When your order is complete, you can expect to receive your prints in the mail within a few days.

Using Photoshop Elements to Order Prints Online

To order prints online using Photoshop Elements, follow these steps:

1 Open the picture or pictures you want to upload in the main work area.

 If you need help opening image files in Photoshop Elements, refer to Chapter 5.

2 From the File menu, choose **Online Services**.

3 Choose one of the available services and click **Next**. When you're logged on to the service's Web site, follow the onscreen instructions.

 If you are prompted to view a license agreement, and you agree to the terms, click **Agree** to continue the ordering process.

Using Picture It! to Order Prints Online

To order prints online using Picture It!, follow these steps:

1 After you've opened the pictures you want to upload, choose **Print Professionally Online** from the **File** menu, and then choose **Prints and Enlargements**.

 If you need help opening image files in Picture It!, refer to Chapter 5.

More About . . . Ordering Prints Online

You can use your Internet browser to go directly to any online printing service and upload your pictures. You can also check the printing and shipping charges, review the turnaround time, and get detailed instructions on how to use the service. The steps vary from service to service, but they should be fairly easy to follow if you use the links at the site.

---

2 In the Prints and Enlargements task pane on the left side of your screen, specify whether you want to print the currently selected picture or all open pictures, and then click Next.

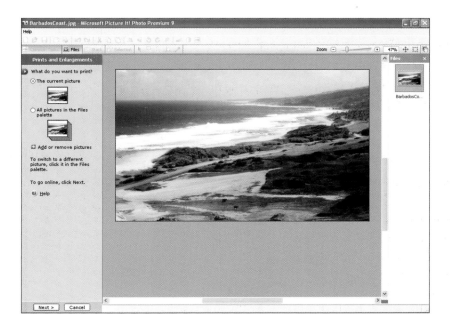

3 There are a variety of services available, including cards, posters, and clothing. Choose the type of project you want from the screen that appears. When you're finished, click Done.

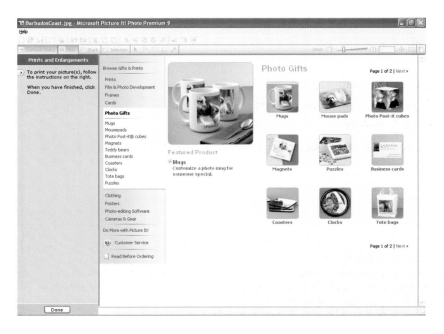

Sharing and Enjoying Your Images

In the old days of film-based cameras, sharing pictures with friends and relatives around the globe involved paying for duplicate prints from your photo shop, not to mention shelling out for postage. This process wasn't terribly burdensome if you only wanted to send a single print to your sister in Nebraska. However, sharing photos of your newborn daughter with every person in your address book was another story altogether.

With digital photography, all that has changed. Thanks to the Internet, you can share your digital photos with as many people as you'd like by e-mailing them, using an online chat program, using an online photo service, or even creating your own Web site. You save time and money, and your friends can save your pictures of Junior to their computer desktops.

Preparing Images for the Internet

Before you use the Internet to share your digital photos with others, consider that the files containing digital images can be quite large, which means they can take a while to download via e-mail or to display properly on a Web site. This is especially true if the person you're sharing your digital photos with uses a dial-up modem to get online rather than a much faster cable modem or DSL (Digital Subscriber Line) connection.

For this reason, it's a good idea to try to keep file size to a minimum when you're sharing digital photos online. One way to do this is to save your digital photos using a lower-quality setting. This reduces the image's resolution, thereby reducing file size. You learned about resolution and quality settings in Chapter 2. Besides, your recipients won't be able to notice the difference when they view the image onscreen. In fact, most images on the Web are at 72 pixels per inch (ppi), whereas print-quality images are around 300 ppi or greater.

 You may be familiar with the term dpi (dots per inch), which also refers to image resolution. The term dpi is used to indicate the resolution of printed images. For example, a printer might be capable of printing 1200 dpi, which means there are 1200 dots of ink for every square inch in the final printed image.

If you've already photographed or scanned the image you want to share, try saving the image file at a lower resolution. For example, try reducing a file with a resolution of 1024×768 to 640×480. The smaller image file usually will retain image quality that rivals the original when viewed onscreen, but it will take much less time to download to a computer. Be sure to check your image-editing application's documentation for the specifics on changing an image's resolution.

This chapter provides detailed steps for tasks using Photoshop Elements and Picture It!. If you use a different program, check its user guide for specific instructions.

In addition to reducing the image's resolution to enable your recipient to download it quickly, you should also consider the image file's format. If you send an image file that uses a format your recipients' image-editing software can't read, they won't be able to view your photograph.

Fortunately, as you learned in Chapter 4, most image-editing programs allow you to save images in a variety of file formats. Even so, it's a good idea to use one of the more common formats to share your images. The JPEG format is a good option because most image-editing software can read it. As an added benefit, it reduces the image's file size while retaining its quality. In fact, most Web pages and e-mail messages that contain images use the JPEG format.

 If you're sending several pictures via e-mail, consider compressing them into a folder rather than sending them separately. Chapter 4 covered compressing images in detail.

E-mailing Your Pictures

The easiest and most common way to share pictures online is to e-mail them. Using e-mail to send your digital photos is free, easy, and instantaneous.

Before you can e-mail digital pictures, you must have an Internet connection and an e-mail account, as well as a program installed on your computer for sending and receiving e-mail. If your computer is running Windows XP, you already have an e-mail program—Outlook Express. Some image-editing software enables you to e-mail pictures from within the program itself. You still must have an e-mail program installed on your PC to do this; the image-editing program uses that program to create the e-mail message for you.

E-mailing with Outlook Express

To e-mail a digital photo using Outlook Express and most other e-mail programs, you simply add the image file to an e-mail message as an attachment. To do so, follow these steps:

 These steps assume you use Outlook Express as your default e-mail program. If you use some other e-mail program, consult its Help options or any documentation you might have to find out how to send files as attachments.

1. Start Outlook Express by clicking **start** and then **E-mail**. The Outlook Express window will open.
2. Click the **Create Mail** button on the toolbar. The New Message window will open.
3. Type the recipient's e-mail address in the **To** field.

4. Type any additional recipients' e-mail addresses in the **To** or **Cc** fields. Be sure to type a comma before each additional address.
5. Type the subject of your message in the **Subject** field.
6. Click in the message area and type any text you want to include.
7. Click the **Attach** button on the toolbar. The Insert Attachment dialog box will open.

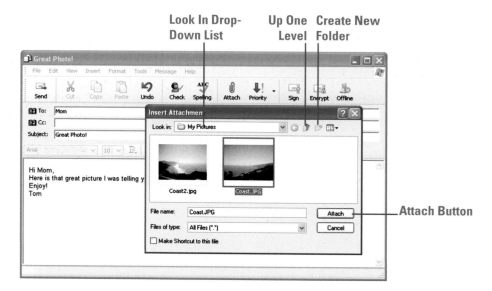

8. Use the **Look in** drop-down list and double-click on folders in the folder list to navigate to the drive and folder that contain your image.
9. Click the folder you want and then click **Open** to display its files.
10. Click the image file you want to attach.
11. Click **Attach**. The name of the image file you've attached will appear in your message's Attach text field.

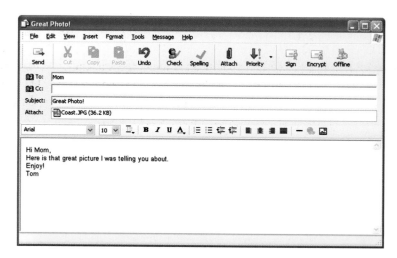

⑫ Click **Send**. If you're connected to the Internet, the message will be sent, and a copy of it will be placed in the Sent Items file.

⑬ If you're not connected to the Internet, the message will be placed in your Outbox. When you're ready to send it, connect to the Internet and click **Send/Recv** on the toolbar.

E-mailing with Picture It!

You can use Picture It! to edit your image and then send it via e-mail directly from the program. (For more information about editing your images, see Chapter 5.) To e-mail a picture using Picture It!, follow these steps:

① Open the picture or pictures you want to send in Picture It! and make any changes you want.

② From the File menu, choose **Send in E-mail**. The Send in E-mail pane will appear on the left.

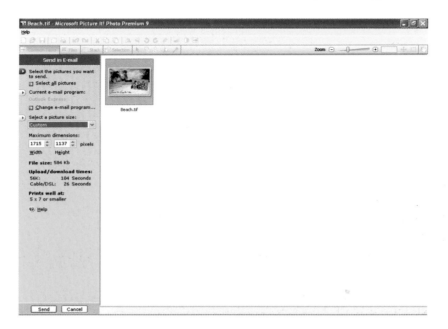

③ Here, choose pictures you want to send, specify the e-mail program, and adjust the image size.

④ Use the **Select a picture size** drop-down menu to specify either the file size or how long it should take the recipient to download the file. These settings are linked; by selecting a small file size, you decrease the download time. Likewise, if you choose a large file size, the download time will increase.

⑤ Click **Send**. Picture It! will create a message in your default e-mail program (in this case, Outlook Express) with the image file attached. The message will include the subject, the attached file, and instructions for viewing the picture.

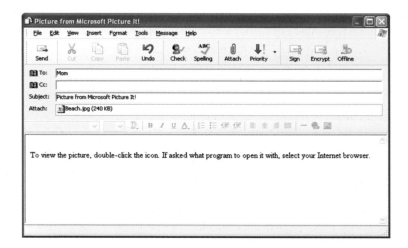

 You also can save the project and e-mail it later if you are not online. Consult Picture It! Help for information on this option.

⑥ Type your recipients' addresses in **To** field.

⑦ Click **Send**. If you're connected to the Internet, the message will be sent immediately. Otherwise, the message will be sent the next time you connect and instruct your e-mail program to send and receive messages.

Sharing Photos Instantly with Windows Messenger

E-mail is great because it enables you to send messages quickly and easily to your friends and family. One drawback of using e-mail, however, is that you might not receive an immediate reply. In fact, depending on how often your recipients check their e-mail, it could be many hours or even days before they respond.

This is where instant-messaging programs are useful. Instant messaging is a way of communicating with friends who are online at the same time you are. Using this type of program, you can have a real-time private conversation, called a chat, with someone, and you can send that person files through this program. Currently, there are several instant-messaging programs available.

If you want to chat and share files with friends online, they must use the same instant-messaging system as you use.

Windows XP comes with a built-in instant-messaging program. This program enables you and other MSN subscribers (or anyone with Windows Messenger installed on his or her desktop) to chat any time you are both online.

More About . . . Setting up Windows Messenger

To set up Windows Messenger on your computer, click start and choose Windows Messenger. Select Click here to sign in to open the .NET Passport Wizard that will guide you through registering your e-mail address with .NET Passport. (If you already have a Hotmail e-mail address, you are already registered.) After you have registered your e-mail address, you will be prompted to sign in with your e-mail address and Passport password. Click Finish to close the wizard and open Windows Messenger. You will be signed in automatically. Click Add a Contact to add someone to your contact list. Look under the Help menu for more details about using Windows Messenger.

Once you have set up your MSN account, you are ready to start sharing your photos using Windows Messenger. Here's how:

1 Click **start**, point to **All Programs**, and then click **Windows Messenger**. The Windows Messenger screen will appear.

2 Click **Send a File or Photo**.

3 Select a contact from the Send a File dialog box, and then click **OK**. The Send a File to <Contact Name> screen will appear.

8

4 Locate the file on your computer that you want to send, and then click **Open**.

5 The Conversation screen will appear, notifying you that the program is waiting for the contact to accept the file. On the other end of the transmission, your online friend must click **Select** for the file to be sent. Once your friend does this, the file will be sent and a delivery confirmation will appear on the Conversation screen.

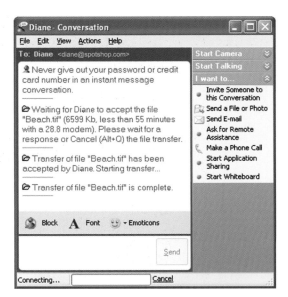

 Instant-messaging programs identify users by their screen names, similar to the way e-mail addresses are used. To find your friends, either ask them for their screen names or use the search feature in your program.

Using Online Photo Services

The Internet plays host to millions of Web sites. Among these are sites designed for digital photographers like you. Using these sites, you can post pictures; get how-to information and ideas for creative photo projects; research reviews and specifications for specific cameras, scanners, accessories; and more. This section discusses the ways you can use online services to share your digital photos.

 Many online photo services also enable you to order prints of your digital images. In fact, many image-editing programs, as well as Windows XP, provide handy links for accessing online printing services and ordering prints. Chapter 7 covered this topic in detail.

Each online photo service operates slightly differently, but you can get an idea of what these sites offer by visiting the Ofoto site. Here's how:

1 Start your Web browser and type **www.ofoto.com** in the address bar.

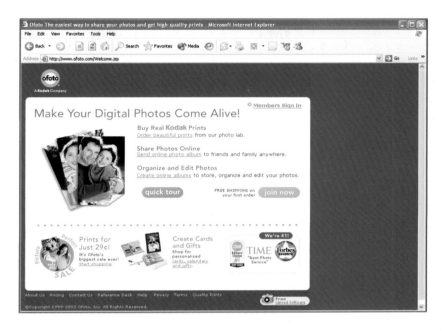

2 If this is your first time visiting Ofoto, you need to set up an account. Click **join now** and follow the instructions. If you already have an account, click **Members Sign In** and type your e-mail address and password.

 Most online photo services require you to set up an account to use their site, which is sometimes free. This typically involves providing your e-mail address, a password, and perhaps a few other details. You also might need to run an installation program to use some of the site's features. Check the instructions for setting up accounts at the site you plan to use.

8

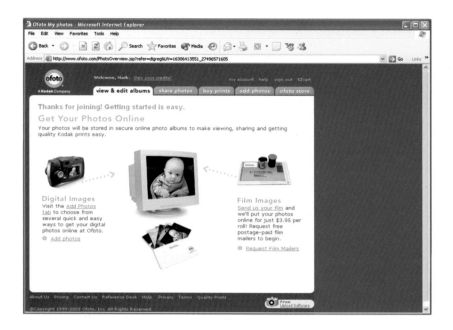

③ The Get Started screen will appear. From here, you can add new pictures, view existing pictures, share pictures online, order prints, create cards, and much more.

 See the next section, "Sharing Pictures Online," for details on adding and sharing pictures.

Sharing Pictures Online

If you want to share only one or two photos with your friends or relatives, e-mailing the photos is usually the best way to go. If you want to share an entire album full of photos, however, e-mailing them can be time-consuming—especially for your recipients. After all, if downloading a single image file is time-consuming, downloading a dozen or more could take hours.

That's where online photo services come in. By posting your images on an online photo service's Web site, you can share as many photos as you'd like with whomever you want. Instead of sending your images to others, you invite your friends and relatives to view your page on the photo service's site. As an added benefit, many online photo services enable visitors to order prints of the photos they've been invited to view.

There are a few ways to post your photos on an online photo service's site. One is to go directly through the site itself; another is to use your image-editing program to post to the site. In the section that follows, you'll learn how to post images to MSN Photos Plus.

Posting Pictures on MSN Photos Plus

To post pictures on MSN Photos Plus, follow these steps:

1 Open your Web browser and type **photos8.msn.com** in the address bar. The MSN Photos page will appear.

2 MSN Photos Plus is a subscription service, so you will need to click **Subscribe Now** and follow the instructions to become a member.

 To post pictures on MSN Photos Plus and access additional features, you will be asked to download and install MSN 8 Internet software in addition to subscribing to MSN Photos Plus. When you do this, you will continue to use your existing ISP for Internet access.

3 After you've become a member, click **Share Photos** and follow the instructions to post the photos you want to share. MSN Photos Plus will send an e-mail message with a link to your online pictures to all the recipients you've entered. The recipients can click this link to view your pictures online.

 By default, your recipients can download and print any shared photos and order prints and photo gifts. You can disable these downloading and printing capabilities if you don't want to grant your recipients permission to do this. Consult the site's Help area for details.

Creating an Online Photo Gallery

If you've photographed a special occasion, such as a baby shower or a graduation ceremony, you might like to organize your images into an album to share online. Several image-editing programs, including Picture It!, enable you to group a set of photos into a project or album and customize how they look, choosing from several designs (as you learned in Chapter 6). Photoshop Elements also includes an option to automatically generate a Web gallery, such as the one shown in Figure 8-1, using all photos stored in a specific folder. To do this, choose **Create Web Photo Gallery** from the File menu. Specify the source and destination folder and click **OK**.

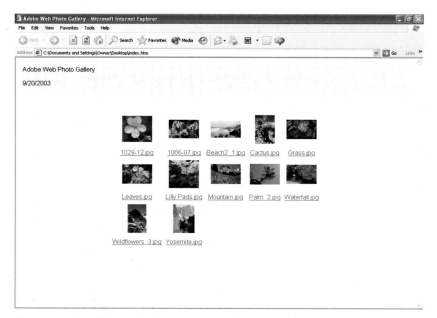

Figure 8-1 Use Photoshop Elements to create a Web gallery automatically.

After you've created a photo album, you can upload it easily to an online photo service site to share with your friends and relatives. To do so, simply follow your online photo service's steps for uploading albums.

Creating Your Own Web Site

Using an online photo service site is a great way to share your photos with others. However, due to limitations, there's not much room for customization when it comes to the way your photos are displayed. If you want to display photos of your best friend's wedding, for example, you might want to add a special background to the page, noting the date of the ceremony and the names of the bride and groom. Most online photo service sites don't allow for this type of customization.

Fortunately, with a little time and effort—not to mention some special software on your computer—you can create your own Web pages. Then you can display your photos any way you want, using any color background, adding text, and even adding links to other sites if you choose, as shown in Figure 8-2.

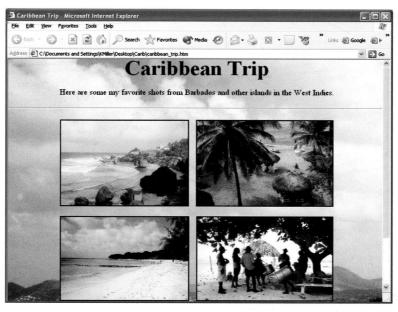

Figure 8-2 Create your own Web page to display your photos any way you like.

Of course, Web publishing is a book topic of its own—there are too many options and programs to cover here. The following list, however, gives you an idea of what tools you'll need to publish to the Web and how best to use digital images on your Web pages.

- ✦ To create your own Web site, you need a program for creating Web pages. Popular programs include Microsoft FrontPage®, Macromedia® Dreamweaver®, and Adobe GoLive®. These programs offer a wide range of tools for both beginners and experienced Web-page designers.

- To publish a Web page, you must have a Web service provider or Web host, which acts as remote storage for your online files. Many of these services are free, but there might be a maximum size limit for your site.

- Most Web pages contain a combination of text, links, and images. A link is a page element that a site visitor can click to quickly access another page on your site or an entirely new site. Programs for creating Web pages include easy ways to insert links.

- Keep the images you include on your page small so they won't take forever to open on visitors' screens. Also, to ensure that all visitors to your Web site will be able to view your images, use an image file format that their browsers will be able to read, such as JPEG.

- The process for inserting images into Web pages depends on the program you use to create the pages. Typically, however, you click **Insert** and then **Picture**, or something similar. After you've added the image to your page, you can resize it and move it as needed.

What's Next in Digital Photography

Based on the progress of digital photography over the past few years, you can expect the field to grow even more exciting in the near future. The popularity of digital cameras is a hint of what's to come. The number of digital cameras sold in North America recently surpassed the number of traditional camera sales. Such a high demand for this technology will likely fuel production of cameras with more features, better image sensors, and a lower price tag.

Here are some features you can find on some of the latest digital camera models:

- New sensor technology is adding even more sharpness to digital images. By capturing full color for every pixel, Foveon's X3 sensor can capture images in greater detail than standard CCD image sensors.

✦ Camera manufacturers have recently unveiled single-use digital cameras. For a nominal fee, you can purchase one of these devices, take about 25 photos, and return the camera for processing. A small processing fee generally gets you traditional 4×6 prints and a CD containing the digital images.

✦ Some new digital cameras feature an OLED (Organic Light Emitting Diode) display that improves upon the common LCD display in several ways. Without the need for backlighting, these screens consume less power, which gives the camera extended battery life. OLED monitors offer higher levels of brightness and sharpness and have a viewing angle up to 165 degrees, as demonstrated in Figure 8-3. The viewing angle is the degree to which you can tilt the screen before the image in no longer visible.

Figure 8-3 OLED displays have a viewing angle far greater than their LCD counterparts.

Of course, higher resolution, more storage capacity, and other improvements to existing features will continue to reshape and improve digital photography. Some predict that in the near future, cameras will produce images with greater detail than traditional film and will have the capacity to double as digital camcorders. In addition to improvements to digital cameras, photo printers, scanners, and image-editing software will pave the way for better-looking images and easier conversion from prints to digital images and vice versa. There has never been a more exciting time to take advantage of digital photography, and the best is yet to come!

8

Glossary

aperture The opening in a camera lens through which light passes to produce an image.

arrays Sensors in digital cameras that convert light information from the scene being photographed into a digital image. See also charge coupled device.

automatic A setting available on some cameras that automatically sets the focus, f-stop, and depth of field. See also focus, f-stop, and depth of field.

battery compartment The slot on a camera where the batteries are stored.

bit Color information is stored in bits; the more bits, the better the range of colors represented.

BMP Stands for Microsoft Bitmap Format. This is the format used for Microsoft Paint. BMP files can be up to 16.8 million colors and are larger than JPEG files.

camera option buttons Buttons on a digital camera that enable the user to move among camera commands or pictures stored in the camera's memory.

CD-R A write-once form of CD media. If you have a CD-R drive, you can write data to CD-R media, but you can only write to CD-R media once. Once a CD-R media is burned, it can be read in any type of CD or DVD drive.

CD-ROM A CD or a CD-ROM media is a read-only CD (hence the name ROM or read only memory). This means you can only read data from the CD; you cannot write data to the CD. Any type of CD or DVD drive can read CD-ROM media.

CD-RW A write-many-times form of CD media. If you have a CD-RW drive, you can write data to CD-R or CD-RW media. You can still only write once to a CD-R media, but you can write, erase, or write data onto CD-RW media again and again. Once a CD-RW media is

burned, it can be read in any type of CD or DVD drive.

charge coupled device (CCD) A light sensor in a digital camera.

CompactFlash One commonly used media card. See also memory card.

composition The organization of subject and background in a photograph; the way you compose your image.

compression The act of reducing a file in size, commonly without noticeable loss in image quality.

connection port An interface on a computer to which you can connect devices with cables, plugs, and other connectors.

CPU (Central Processing Unit) The main processor chip on a computer's motherboard—not the whole system unit. It interprets and carries out instructions, performs computations, and controls the devices connected to the computer.

cradle When set in a cradle connected to your computer, usually with a USB or FireWire connection, a digital camera can be recharged, and images on the device can be managed from your computer.

crop To remove a portion of an image.

cutout A region cropped from an image, usually to be pasted into another image. The boundaries of the cutout area are either drawn manually or selected with an image-editing program's automatic selection tools.

depth of field The area of a picture that is in sharp focus.

digital album Like a conventional photo album, a way to present and arrange pictures in an order you choose.

digital image Any image that has been created by a source, such as a digital camera, and converted electronically to be viewed on screen. See also pixel and scanner.

digital zoom A feature of some digital cameras that mimics optical zoom. With digital zoom, the camera photographs an entire scene but saves only a portion of it or expands a portion by adding pixels. The same effect can be obtained using an image-editing program. See also optical zoom.

docking station A component that can be attached to a computer to transfer images from a digital camera to the computer more easily.

download To copy images from a digital camera to a computer. Also refers to copying files from the Internet to a computer.

dpi (dots per inch) The standard measurement of resolution used with printed images. Generally, a higher dpi indicates higher resolution. See also resolution.

driver A file that tells the Windows operating system the details of a particular hardware component, such as a printer, digital camera, or scanner. When the component is installed on a computer, a driver for it is copied to the computer.

DVD A DVD media is a read-only DVD. You can play a movie DVD in your home theater DVD player or in the DVD drive on your computer. This type of media holds a minimum of 4.7GB (gigabytes), enough for a full-length movie.

DVD-R A write-once form of DVD media. A DVD-R media is a DVD media that can be written to once. A DVD-R or DVD-RAM drive is required to write to DVD-R media. Once a DVD-R is burned, it can be read in any type of DVD drive.

DVD+R/DVD+RW Media comparable in functionality to DVD-R and DVD-RW designed for burning with a DVD+R/DVD+RW compatible drive. DVD+R/DVD+RW formats are supported by an alliance of computer manufacturers and are not officially recognized by the DVD forum (an international association of hardware and software manufacturers who promote broad acceptance of DVD products).

DVD-RAM DVD-RAM is a leading standard for recording images and data to DVDs. A DVD-RAM drive can read information on DVDs and write information to DVD-RAM discs, which can be written to multiple times.

effective pixels The number of pixels on an image sensor that are read while taking a picture with a digital camera. This is the actual resolution measurement of a digital camera.

EXIF (Extended File Format) A format used by digital cameras to store additional information, such as the date, time, or whether the flash was used, along with the image data. This data can be accessed while editing the image.

exposure The process of exposing a camera's image sensor or film to light to create an image. Exposure is affected by settings such as focus, aperture, and shutter speed.

file format The method used to store data in a file. Different programs can open and work with different file formats. Popular formats for digital image files include JPEG and TIFF. See also JPEG and TIFF.

film scanner A scanner used to convert negatives and slides into digital files. See also scanner.

FireWire A method of connecting a computer to peripherals including external storage devices, such as portable digital music players, external sound cards, and other devices. To use a FireWire connection requires a FireWire port on the computer, an external device that supports FireWire, and a compatible cable.

flash A device used to produce a bright flash of light to illuminate the subject of a photograph.

flatbed scanner A scanner that converts text or images into digital files using a moving light source similar to that used by a copier. Flatbed scanners are the most common type of scanner. See also scanner.

focal length The distance between a camera lens and the image the lens creates. A shorter focal length creates a wider angle of view, whereas a longer focal length creates a narrower angle of view focusing in on the subject of the photograph.

focus Adjustment of the distance setting on a lens to define the subject sharply. This can be done automatically or manually.

f-stop A manual setting whereby the diameter of the aperture is adjusted to change the depth of field. See also depth of field and aperture.

GIF A digital image file format used mostly for Web graphics.

gigabyte (GB) A unit of computer memory or data storage capacity equal to 1,024 megabytes.

handheld scanner A small device primarily used to scan text.

hard drive The internal storage device responsible for storing your operating system, programs, images, and other files.

image-editing program A program that enables the user to view, edit, and print digital images.

inkjet printer A printer that works by spraying a fine, quick-drying ink onto paper.

JPEG (Joint Photographic Experts Group) A file format often used for pictures posted on the World Wide Web.

laser printer A printer that uses a laser beam to burn toner on paper.

LCD (Liquid Crystal Display) An LCD screen on a digital camera displays pictures and messages.

lens A piece of glass on a camera used to collect and focus rays of light to form an image.

light meter An instrument that measures the exposure of light on a subject.

media card Removable media inserted into a digital camera to provide additional storage space. Pictures stored on a media card can be transferred to a computer or photo printer. See also CompactFlash, Smart Media and SD Card.

media slot A slot in a digital camera into which a media card can be inserted. See also media card.

megabyte (MB) A unit of computer memory or data storage equal to 1,048,576 bytes. In terms of digital images, 1 megabyte is about the disk space required to store one 5×7 inch print-quality digital image.

megapixel One million pixels. Megapixel is the unit used to measure digital camera quality; there are one-, two-, and four-megapixel (and higher) cameras. See also pixel.

memory See RAM.

memory card See media card.

menu button A button on a digital camera that enables the user to access camera commands for setting the date, selecting the resolution, and so on.

mode A setting that affects how a digital camera works. Modes include picture mode, for taking pictures, and playback (review) mode, for reviewing pictures. Mode names vary from camera to camera.

OLED (Organic Light-Emitting Diode) This display technology competes with traditional LCD displays. They are more energy-efficient and offer a wider viewing angle.

open To make an image available to be edited.

operating system The software on your computer responsible for file management and running programs. Windows XP, for example, is an operating system.

optical zoom A lens on a film-based or digital camera that can be used to change the range of space captured by the camera's film or image sensor while keeping the image in focus. See also digital zoom.

overexposing A condition in which too much light reaches the film, resulting in light, undefined images.

PDF (Portable Document Format) PDF files, which can be viewed with Adobe Acrobat Reader, are often used for Web pages and transfer over the Internet.

pixel A tiny dot of light, which is the basic unit of measurement for images on a computer screen or in a digital image.

Plug and Play setup A set of specifications developed by Intel for automatic configuration of a computer to work with various devices, such as digital cameras.

port An opening on the back or front of a computer into which a cable can be plugged to connect a printer, digital camera, or other hardware component. Port types include parallel (or LPT) ports, serial ports, and USB (universal serial bus) ports.

ppi (pictures per inch) The standard measurement of resolution used with scanned images. See also resolution.

printer A device that prints text or graphical images from a computer. A printer can produce black or color output on paper and typically connects to a PC using a parallel or USB port.

PSD (Photoshop Format) This is the native format of Adobe Photoshop and Adobe Photoshop Elements. Files saved in this format can be opened in Photoshop products. Some other image-editing programs are also capable of opening PSD files.

RAM (Random Access Memory) Temporarily stores data, software, and the operating system while a computer is operating. RAM is measured in megabytes (M or MB) or gigabytes (G or GB).

red-eye A common flaw in photographs in which eyes are displayed and printed as red. Most image-editing programs can correct this problem.

resolution The measure of a digital image's quality. For scanners, resolution is measured in ppi. For printers, resolution is measured in dpi.

Generally, a higher dpi indicates higher resolution. For cameras, resolution is measured by megapixel.

rotate To adjust an image. This can be used to correct images that were scanned at an unsatisfactory angle.

save To copy an image to permanent storage. It's a good idea to save your original image and then work from a copy.

scanner A hardware component that can convert documents and pictures into digital files. See also sheet feed scanner, flatbed scanner, film scanner, and handheld scanner.

SD (SansDisk) Card SD media cards are commonly used removable media. See also media card.

sheet feed scanner A scanner that can hold multiple sheets like a printer and is suitable for copying large text documents. See also scanner.

shutter button A button on a camera that the user presses to take a picture. It is almost always on the top of the camera.

shutter speed The amount of time the shutter remains open.

slide shows Presenting pictures where each of the images is displayed full-screen on your computer, one after another.

Smart Media One commonly used media card. See also media card.

tag Information, such as a category or description, assigned to an image that allows you to find it easily using image-management software.

TIFF (Tagged Image File Format) A high-quality digital image format often used for pictures appearing in printed publications.

TWAIN The official technical standard for scanning images. Almost all scanners come with a TWAIN driver.

underexposing A condition in which too little light reaches the film, resulting in dark, undefined images.

USB Stands for universal serial bus. A type of port often used to connect scanners and cameras to a computer.

viewfinder A window on the body of a camera that the user looks through to frame and shoot a photograph.

wizard A Windows feature that leads the user through a process step by step. For example, the Add Scanner or Camera Wizard enables the user to install a new scanner or digital camera.

X3 A type of image sensor that competes with the CCD. This type of sensor claims to produce sharper images by capturing full color for each pixel.

zip archive A file or number of files compressed and packaged into a single file of a smaller file size. In Windows XP, these files usually look like a file with a zipper down the middle, and they can be decompressed by simply moving them out of the compressed folder.

Index